The First-Year Teacher

Fourth Edition

The First-Year Teacher

Be Prepared for Your Classroom

Fourth Edition

Karen A. Bosch

Morghan E. Bosch

CORWIN
A SAGE Company

FOR INFORMATION:

Corwin

A SAGE Company

2455 Teller Road

Thousand Oaks, California 91320

(800) 233-9936

www.corwin.com

SAGE Publications Ltd.

1 Oliver's Yard

55 City Road

London EC1Y 1SP

United Kingdom

SAGE Publications India Pvt. Ltd.

B 1/I 1 Mohan Cooperative Industrial Area

Mathura Road, New Delhi 110 044

India

SAGE Publications Asia-Pacific Pte. Ltd.

3 Church Street

#10-04 Samsung Hub

Singapore 049483

Copyright © 2015 by Corwin

Printed in the United States of America

A catalog record of this book is available from the Library of Congress.

ISBN: 978-1-4833-1771-7

Acquisitions Editor: Jessica Allan

Associate Editor: Kimberly Greenberg

Editorial Assistant: Cesar Reyes

Production Editor: Melanie Birdsall

Copy Editor: Diane DiMura

Typesetter: C&M Digitals (P) Ltd.

Proofreader: Alison Syring

Indexer: Molly Hall

Cover Designer: Gail Buschman

Marketing Manager: Lisa Lysne

CONTENTS

PREFACE

Since we have received such positive feedback from new teachers about this book and we believe the material is timeless, we have decided to revise each chapter and add new information, resources, and teacher experiences. In addition, we have added a chapter (Chapter 3) to help the newly hired special education teacher be prepared for an inclusive classroom and the co-teaching experience.

In this new edition, we have added more recent citations of research done in the field of beginning teachers; more tips for teachers gathered from teachers in the elementary, middle, secondary, and special education classrooms; and feedback received from the many readers of the book over the last few years.

Since assessment has become such a hot topic and teachers are being asked to provide evidence of their teaching effectiveness, we have presented information on teaching with assessment strategies, and planning lessons with assessment as a component. We have added more opportunities for teachers to explore the term *reflection*, as it remains the best process in reaching personal and professional goals of teaching excellence. Improving teacher effectiveness and student learning becomes even more important in the quest for high-stakes accountability, achieving standards of quality in education, and fulfilling the No Child Left Behind (NCLB) legislation as well as the Common Core curriculum.

We hope that by making these revisions to *The First-Year Teacher,* its relevance and helpfulness will become even more evident to the aspiring, beginning, or even seasoned teacher, who wants to improve and ensure effectiveness in the classroom today, tomorrow, and in the future.

Definitions

By *first-year teacher*, we are referring to an educator who is

- new to the profession,
- returning to the profession,
- new to a school district,
- changing grade levels,

- changing from elementary or secondary to middle school level,

- noncertified, or

- a graduate of an alternative teacher preparation program.

In addition, this text can be used for the following:

- Instruction—The text can be used to prepare education students for the classroom and for clinical experiences.

- Remediation—The text provides guidelines to becoming a more effective classroom manager.

- Assistance—The text can guide the efforts of mentor and mentee programs.

- Support—The text can assist administrators in planning in-services and special programs for beginning teachers.

- Guidance—The text can standardize the management procedures at grade level or school level.

Main Features

The First-Year Teacher has several features that make it unique in responding to the challenges of the first year of teaching:

1. This book is unique in that it moves the teacher chapter by chapter through the first year. Chapter 1 prepares a teacher for the job market. Chapter 2 is designed to move the new teacher into the classroom. Chapter 3 is for the special education teacher destined for a co-teaching experience. Chapter 4 should be read before the parents or guardians come to meet you. Teachers need information on how to work with parents or guardians and gain their support. Some of the first opportunities for teachers to meet parents or guardians are at school-scheduled visitation nights, open houses, and parent-or-guardian-teacher conferences. Chapter 5 is considered an on-the-job training program that is a step-by-step classroom management plan for the first month. This chapter can be read day by day during the first thirty days in the classroom. Chapter 6 is designed to promote teacher efficiency and save you time doing your job. It is to be read over the long-awaited winter (holiday) break. Many new teachers have reported that you must spend a few months in the classroom before you can deal with time-saving techniques. Chapter 7 will help you end the first year, be reflective, and prepare for the next teaching year. A college professor using this book in a teacher education program commented that it is nice to have a book that provides a teacher with a dry run of how to begin a school year and takes them through this experience one chapter at a time.

2. The contents of *The First-Year Teacher* are research based. We conducted many studies using surveys designed to identify the problems, concerns, needs, and feelings of first-year teachers. We chose twenty-five newly hired, first-year teachers to field-test the 30-day management plan. These teachers, elementary through high school, met with me several times throughout their first year to strengthen the plan and provide a fresh look at the concerns of a first-year teacher. Each school year, approximately ten first-year teachers volunteered to read the book and use the 30-day management plan. We collected valuable feedback that is reflected in this revised text.

   We feel privileged to have the opportunity to get not only into the heads of new teachers but into their hearts as well. This book and its contents continue to be written for teachers and by teachers, both new and veteran, to help prepare others for the first year of their teaching careers.

3. The emphasis in this book is on teacher preparation for the first year and subsequent years. The book offers suggestions, ideas, and advice from practitioners and experts in the field. It provides lesson plans for accomplishing teaching goals. It shares journal entries and experiences that only a first-year teacher could know, which enables readers to identify with other first-year teachers and with the book's contents. The content is relevant, meaningful, and useful in helping beginning teachers by addressing their fears and frustrations, answering their questions, and giving them hope. It supports the teacher through the first year and from the beginning to the end of the year.

   A teacher who was recently hired to begin her first year reviewed the manuscript and said, "I am reading what I need to know. I think I will call this book my GPS for traveling through my first year."

4. The 30-day—first month—management plan provides a framework that first-year teachers can follow. For some, it can be a checklist of activities to develop concepts and goals through a planned, developmental approach. For others, it can be a map to follow to help them feel less alone and inexperienced.

5. The *First-Year Teacher* serves as a support for first-year teachers in their transition from campus to classroom. It is useful for the career switchers in their move to the classroom. It can help those teachers who are returning to the classroom after an extended period of time. It can offer a fresh beginning for a teacher in need of change. Six first-year teachers were asked to keep journals, and their journal entries are interspersed throughout the book. Interestingly, classrooms have changed over time; however, the first-year teachers are still saying the same things and expressing some of the same thoughts.

Organization

The general theme for *The First-Year Teacher* is PREPARATION. The book introduces the reader to a range of topics that were identified as essential by first-year teachers. The seven chapters provide new teachers with a plan and a focus for meeting their needs and the students' needs. A coding system in Chapter 5 is another unique feature of this book and was developed specifically for teachers working in special education, middle school, secondary, and culturally diverse classrooms. This coding system allows the teacher quick access to classroom-specific information:

- ✤ **special education**
- ✦ **middle school**
- ★ **secondary**
- ✳ **culturally diverse learners**

The codes make it easier for a teacher to access specific strategies and tailor the 30-day management plan to meet specific classroom needs and student challenges.

Many beginning teachers have expressed the need for one more college course or text to prepare future teachers for the transition from campus to classroom. It is our hope that this book will provide the missing link between teacher preparation programs and the first-year teaching experience, as well as the crucial link between teacher effectiveness and improved student learning.

ABOUT THE AUTHORS

 **Karen A. Bosch**, PhD, is a professor of education at Virginia Wesleyan College. Dr. Bosch is the coordinator of the Education Department and the director of teacher education at Virginia Wesleyan College. She is the recipient of the Virginia Wesleyan College's Batten Distinguished Faculty Award for excellence in teaching, scholarship, and having a passion for inspiring others. Most recently, she received the Samuel Nelson Gray Distinguished Teaching Award recognizing those who set the pace of excellence. Dr. Bosch has written *The First-Year Teacher* (1994, 2000, 2010) and *Planning Classroom Management for Change* (1999, 2006). As an educational consultant, she has conducted seminars and workshops on classroom management, lesson planning, and effective classroom teaching. She has presented her research and her teacher preparation programs models at conferences nationwide. Dr. Bosch is a former public school teacher and administrator.

 **Morghan E. Bosch**, BS, MS, CAGS, is a special education teacher in the Virginia Beach City Public School System and an adjunct instructor at Virginia Wesleyan College. Ms. Bosch is currently in the dissertation phase of her doctoral program in special education at Regent University. In addition to *The First-Year Teacher*, Ms. Bosch has written a chapter, "Literacy in K–12 Content Courses," in the book *Beach Ball Banter* (2012) and coauthored *The Autism Guide for Norfolk Public Schools* (2009). She has given numerous presentations, such as "Social Skills and Children With Learning Disabilities" (2012), "Vocational Preparation for Students with Autism" (2013), and "Autism and Employment" (2013). Ms. Bosch started *Beach Buddies*, an extracurricular program that partners special education students with general education peers to create mutual friendships. She has received the School Bell Award and Community Service Inspiration Award for building connections between the community and special education population.

CHAPTER ONE

Where Do I Start?

I. The Application Process

The graduate faces many challenges in beginning a teaching career and must start the job search as early as possible. The first step to getting a job is to secure and complete applications. You need to determine which school systems are of interest to you. Check out the school system's website, and complete the application online. If the application is not online, call the school system and ask to have the application sent to you or pick it up in person. Make a copy of the original application form and prepare a rough draft. Next, transfer the information to the original application and send or deliver it in person. Choose your references carefully. Contact them to get their permission and discuss with them your future plans.

Set Up a Credential File

Use word processing software to create an electronic credential file. Be sure to update it regularly to reflect new information and experiences. Collect or create the following items:

1. Transcript(s)

2. Two-page résumé

3. Names and addresses of possible employers/teachers/friends who will be good references

4. Letters of recommendation

5. List of work experiences, both paid and volunteer

6. Detailed descriptions of a few work experiences involving teaching or activities working with children

7. List of achievements, awards, and extracurricular activities

8. Assessment scores on required state tests, such as Praxis tests

9. Philosophy statement

10. Sample lesson plan

11. Brief classroom management plan

12. Plan for technology use, including the integration of technology into teaching, use of computers in the classrooms, and a plan for scheduling

Set Up a School System File

You need to be informed about each of the school systems to which you are applying. It is time to do some homework. Attempt to contact someone who is presently teaching or working within the school system. Also, try to find out the names of people who have also made applications to the same school systems. Contact them and form a network of job seekers to aid each other in securing a job. (Later, this could be a supportive network of first-year teachers.) Sharing information pertaining to the interview process, and the questions that were asked, can add a measure of confidence to a scary experience. There are some questions below that you may wish to ask the person working in the school systems you have chosen. Take notes, as this information may be useful during the interview process.

- What do you like about this school system or the school to which you are assigned?

- If you could change one thing about your job, what would it be?

- Do you feel that your school administration is supportive?

- Would you say your school system is conservative, innovative, or behind the times?

- What is the latest innovation or curricular change being implemented in the schools?

- Tell me about your reading program?

- I am applying for a position in your school system. Do you have any advice for me?

Visit the websites of the school systems and review information found there to help you generate some questions you may want to ask during the interview. Make a list of interesting facts gleaned from previewing the school systems' sites. Use a database program to create an electronic file for each school system to which you have applied. The file may contain the following items:

1. Copy of completed application

2. List of the individuals contacted who are presently teaching or working in the system; include the notes from the conversations

3. List of people who are also applying to this school system and their phone numbers

4. List of sample interview questions

5. Summary of points of interest

II. Preparing a Résumé and a Portfolio

A résumé is many things to many people. It can represent a first impression, a summary of life experiences, an autobiography, a paper profile, and more. It is a written portrait of you on paper. An educator's résumé is different from résumés that are written for most other occupations. It will contain vocabulary that is unique to education, classroom teaching, and student learning.

Writing a Résumé

To write a résumé, a preservice teacher must present biographical information, provide educational qualifications, and highlight teaching experience. Specific information, such as the number of hours in field experience, volunteer situations, and community service activities, must be collected. Next, the preservice teacher needs to describe the specific tasks that were involved in working with people, children, and supervisors. Begin thinking about the skills and abilities utilized in employment positions, field experiences, and extracurricular activities. Reflect on past work tasks and responsibilities and think of describing those experiences using words such as *designing*, *preparing*, *developing*, and *implementing* projects and activities. Think about the skills developed when you conducted meetings and when you had to create, write, and report information. Describe details of these experiences by including such verbs as *summarize*, *analyze*, and *evaluate*. Share your experiences facilitating group activities and working with small and large groups. Supply information about the conferences you may have attended. Think about your competencies, personal qualities, and professional strengths, and highlight them in your résumé. See Figure 1.1 for items to include in your résumé. Zukergood and Bettencourt (2009) suggest that you start from your most recent experiences and work backward, organizing your résumé by sections. They also suggest proofreading your résumé and sending a cover letter with it. The book *101 Grade A Résumés for Teachers* by Anthony and Roe (2003) and *Resumes for Education Careers* (VGM Career Horizons, 2004) are excellent resources.

The best advice for résumé writing is to keep it simple and short—if possible, no longer than two pages. Organize it carefully, make it easy to read, and remember that appearance is important. Always ask a reader or two to proof your résumé before you mail, e-mail, or take it to an interview. Be prepared to leave a résumé with the interviewer.

FIGURE 1.1 *Items to Include in Your Résumé*

Competencies

Knowledge in subject area

Ability to motivate learning

Ability to differentiate learning

Sensitivity to needs of learners

Working with children of varying ages and abilities

Working with children of different cultural backgrounds

Personal Qualities	*Professional Strengths*
Leadership ability	Familiarity with professional literature
Willingness to learn	Strong communication skills
Fairness	Professional experiences with children other
Flexibility	than student teaching
Positivity	
Team player	

Many articles and example résumés are found in the American Association for Employment in Education (AAEE) book ***AAEE Job Search Handbook for Educators*** (2015). That handbook will provide more specific information and, possibly, some answers to lingering questions. See Figure 1.2 for a sample résumé.

FIGURE 1.2 *Résumé*

555 Anywhere Street

Everytown, State 55555

(555) 555–5555 (h)

lastname@hotmail.com

Objective: To secure an elementary teacher position (PreK–6).

Education

College or university, City, State

BA, interdivisional major, May 2014

Certification area—Elementary (PreK–6)

4.0 GPA

Dean's List

Community College, City, State
AA, liberal arts, August 2011
3.754 GPA
President's List

Honors
Kappa Delta Pi International Honors Society of Educators
Spring 2012–present

Related Experiences

May 2014–present   *Substitute teacher—all grades*
                                          School system, City, State

January 2014–May 2014   *Student teacher—Grade 1 and 4*
                                          School system, School, City, State

- Planned and implemented all subject area lesson plans (with special attention paid to differentiation).
- Performed all daily instructional and administrative classroom procedures.
- Implemented and enforced positive classroom management.

September 2012–December 2013   *Practicum student—Grade 2 and 5*
                                          School System, School, City, State

- Planned and implemented lesson plans (with special attention paid to special needs and ESL students).
- Performed daily classroom routines and procedures.
- Implemented classroom management strategies.

Additional Experience

April 2002–January 2008   *Energy team member*

- Researched sporting activities and recreational events to determine sales viability.
- Planned all travel schedules to balance times and increase sales.
- Managed team with the team manager.

Computer Skills
Word Perfect, Windows, InDesign, Excel, MS Word, FilemakerPro, Quark Express, Photoshop, Acrobat Reader, Internet, MS Paint, Rubistar, PowerPoint, MS Access, Portaportal, Smart Board, and QuizStar

Activities
Treasurer, Student Virginia Education Association (SVEA)

Preparing a Portfolio

A portfolio—in a visual way—says more about who you are and what you have to offer than your résumé can. The résumé becomes one part of the portfolio. A professional teaching portfolio is an organized collection of documentation, papers, letters, and pictures that highlight your personal and professional achievements and efforts. Zeichner and Wray (2001, p. 614) state that a portfolio "encourages student teachers to think more deeply about their teaching and about subject matter content, to become more conscious of the theories and assumptions that guide their practices, and to develop a greater desire to engage in collaborative dialogues about teaching."

Tucker, Stronge, & Gareis (2002) view portfolios as tools for self-reflection and professional development. The portfolio's role in reflecting continuous personal growth is further discussed in Chapter 6.

Many new teachers prepare business cards and brochures to be included in their portfolios. See Figure 1.3 for a sample brochure. The portfolio offers you, the beginning teacher, a means of marketing yourself. By providing an interviewer with a close and personal look at you, you are not seen as just a candidate for a teaching position. Many interviewers will not ask to see your portfolio. Suggest to the interviewer that you would like to highlight a few items from your portfolio.

Developing a Portfolio

It seems natural to expect an artist to open a large black art portfolio to show samples of artwork when interviewing for an art position or applying for entry into an art show. A portfolio for a preservice teacher is a compilation of teaching evidence that can document professional commitment, preservice teaching experience, and classroom efforts. It is a snapshot of your professional development to date. You will want to begin early to collect pictures, ideas, materials, and samples of students' work from early field experiences. Zukergood and Bettencourt (2009, pp. 193–195) suggest gathering artifacts for your portfolio while you are student teaching. When it is time to organize your portfolio, you will need to reflect on the collected material and decide what to include. Choose the most important or current ideas, events, and experiences that capture who you are and define you as a teacher. Zubizarreta (1994) suggests that a portfolio is "an evidence-based document that combines selective information from a variety of sources and that presents a vigorous and factual profile of an individual teacher's effort, the portfolio authenticates contemporary discourse about the scholarship of teaching" (p. 327).

Portfolio Organization

Portfolios are like personal scrapbooks, but even more, they define and reveal much about the maker as a person and a teacher. It gives you an opportunity to be creative

FIGURE 1.3 Sample Brochure

Head Shot

Experience

- Practicum experience in an early elementary school setting
- Practicum experience in an upper elementary setting in a hard-to-staff school
- Student teaching experience in first grade at school system, school, city, state
- Student teaching experience in fourth grade at school system, school, city, state

Contact Information

Jane M. Doe
555 Anywhere Street
Everytown, State 55555

Home phone
(555) 555-5555

Cell phone
(555) 555-5555

E-mail
lastname@hotmail.com

Jane M. Doe

Teacher Certification:
Pre K–6

Teaching is one of the noblest professions. It requires an adequate preparation and training, patience, devotion, and a deep sense of responsibility. Those who mold the human mind have wrought not for time, but for eternity.

–Calvin Coolidge

About Me

I decided to become a teacher because of my desire to be a lifelong learner and my love of children. I can think of nothing more rewarding than helping to shape young children's lives and imparting upon them a thirst for knowledge. I believe learning should be fun and I challenge myself to create fun and exciting lessons for my students.

Professional Goals

- Work together with parents and guardians, fellow teachers, students, and administration to hone my teaching craft
- Obtain my masters of education degree
- Attend teacher development courses in all subjects to continue to advance my teaching methods

(Continued)

FIGURE 1.3   *Sample Brochure*

Continued

My Philosophy

Teaching is not about dictating to students. I do not believe in simply giving worksheets and testing students. Learning should be fun. All material can and should be covered but in a creative way that engages both student and teacher. Students should be encouraged to explore and learn through discovery. Learning through exploration has proven to create better retention in learners, both young and old. My belief is that a teacher's role is that of a guide and facilitator. Students

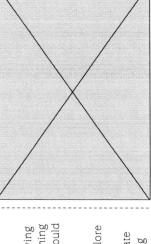

need to work together in small groups and work cooperatively and collaboratively. In this type of environment, students learn from one another. A successful classroom begins with a teacher who gives students the tools to become critical thinkers and problem solvers. These skills will continue to serve these students for the rest of their lives.

My Teaching Goals

- Impart the love of knowledge onto children so they will become lifelong learners
- Create a positive classroom environment that is a safe place for students to learn
- Create a learning community that involves students, parents and guardians, fellow teachers, administration, and the community
- Allow students the freedom to explore concepts and ideas
- Allow children to believe they are special and can be successful

Technology Experience

- Smart Board
- Computer programs (Kidspiration, Inspiration, etc.)

and unique. Organization of your portfolio is important, and you must think carefully about how to present it. It must be succinct, yet comprehensive. Allan May, in the ***AAEE Job Search Handbook for Educators*** (1997, p. 18), presents the following table of contents for a portfolio:

1. Résumé

2. Transcripts, national examination results, and state certification documents

3. Evidence of community involvement

4. Evidence of people/student orientation

5. Classroom performance

6. Directing of extracurricular activities

7. Evidence that you are a lifelong learner

8. Evidence of teamwork

You can find more information on developing portfolios in ***How to Develop a Professional Portfolio: A Manual for Teachers*** (Campbell, Melenzyer, Nettles, & Wyman, 2013).

The two most important elements of a portfolio are appearance and format. Eye appeal and ease of reviewing the portfolio make an impression. Portfolios that are organized and user friendly are remembered. You should have an electronic version of your portfolio as well as a hard copy ready for distribution. If you are presenting a hard copy version, place your portfolio in a flat binder and label sections for easy identification.

The portfolios scored highest by interviewers included the following sections:

A. Personal—Basic Contact Information

   1. Title page that includes your name, address, phone number, and e-mail address

   2. Cover letter of introduction and explaining the format of your portfolio

   3. Table of Contents

B. Preparation Materials—Evidence of Academic Scholarship: Specific items to include are

   1. Statement of personal and professional philosophy of teaching (i.e., short- and long-term professional goals; teaching philosophy statement(s); poem or slogan, with explanations, which happens to be meaningful to you)

   2. Résumé

3. Transcripts

4. Honors and recognitions

5. Assessment tests scores, such as Praxis tests

C. Commitment to Teaching and Evidence of Teaching Competence

1. Summary of course work taken and how it relates to your competence

2. Summary of field experiences and cooperating teachers' evaluations, administrators' evaluations, college supervisors' evaluations

3. Additional letters of recognition, recommendations from various sources

4. Self-evaluations, reflective journal entries

5. Pictures of students' work, projects, bulletin boards

6. Sample lesson plans, thematic units

7. Evidence of innovative lessons (use of technology, cooperative learning activities, etc.)

8. Technology portfolio or examples of technology skills on removable media

The electronic portfolio is increasingly becoming a part of the interview process. The electronic portfolio provides not only an assessment of the candidate's technological sophistication but also an opportunity for the evaluator to see evidence of your technology skills.

D. Evidence of Classroom Management Competence

1. Classroom management plan

2. Examples of classroom management lesson plans

A classroom management plan is outlined in the book **Planning Classroom Management** (Bosch, 2006). The book presents an observation guide that assists the preservice teacher in collecting classroom management information from early field and student teaching experiences. The collected data then are used to develop a classroom management plan. Bosch discusses how a classroom management plan provides interviewers with the assurance that they are hiring both a first-year teacher and an experienced teacher (p. viii). Beyond a doubt, a documented classroom management plan takes some of the risk out of hiring first-year teachers.

The portfolio provides a personal tool for reflecting upon your teaching skills, knowledge, and understanding. It reflects your growth and changes as a preservice teacher and provides a foundation for introspection and goal setting. The portfolio is an evolving document. It is being endorsed at both the state and national levels for preservice and practicing teachers as a way to assess and document successful teaching.

III. Preparing for the Interview

When you have an interview date, immediately do more homework. Pick out the appropriate file and review your application responses. Check out the school's website again for current information. Contact your network people to gain information and inquire whether or not they have had an interview. If so, ask about the interview process and the questions that were asked. Plan a trial drive to the school administration building or school where the interview is to take place so that you can plan the appropriate amount of driving time to ensure arriving on time. Arriving early would even be better. Review sample interview questions and practice reciting your answers to them. Use some of your education textbooks to review key concepts and practices, as well as theorists' names that can be used to add strength to your responses.

It is important that you plan to take an active part in the interview process. Decide on questions you will ask the interviewer(s). Prepare specific information that you will emphasize during your interview, such as your accomplishments and recognitions. Write short paragraphs containing such information. Rehearse speaking the written information. Role-play an interview. As one beginning teacher suggested, "Rehearse in the shower." You may want to keep a journal to reflect upon the interview experiences.

Sample questions that may be asked by interviewers include the following:

1. Describe your most rewarding teaching experience.

2. If I walked into your classroom during math, what would I see?

3. How would you handle a child who is constantly disrupting the class?

4. How would you manage behavior in your classroom?

5. How would you motivate your students?

6. What are the strengths you bring to teaching?

7. How would you establish communication with parents or guardians?

8. How would you provide differentiated learning experiences for your students?

9. In your classroom, if there is a child who never completes assignments or a child who finishes work quickly and correctly, what would you do?

10. How would you assess student progress?

See Figure 1.4 for more interview questions.

The interview date has arrived. Dress professionally and be enthusiastic, friendly, and polite. Sit tall and make eye contact. Take a few seconds to think about each question before you begin the response. If you are not sure of an answer

FIGURE 1.4   *More Interview Questions*

All questions have been forwarded by first-year teachers to increase the preparedness for the job interview.

- Tell me about yourself.

- Describe the best teacher you have known.

- What are your long-range career plans?

- Why have you selected education as a profession?

- What was a highlight of your student teaching experience(s)?

- How would your students describe you?

- Describe an experience teaching a minority student.

- Explain your style of teaching.

- Describe what I would see if I walked into your classroom.

- Tell me a classroom management theorist you plan to use in your classroom and why.

- Explain the teaching strategies that have been most successful for you.

- What strategies are you planning to use to promote critical thinking?

- What is your grading philosophy?

- How do you think you can contribute to our school system?

Some special education-specific questions:

- How would you work in an inclusion setting?

- Summarize the IEP process.

Some middle school-specific questions:

- How can you make peer pressure positive?

- What are some management ideas for grouping students?

- How do you deal with a student that constantly acts up in your classroom?

- How can teaming work best?

Some secondary-specific questions:

- English—Name a British or American author who has had a strong impact on literature.

- History—What war do you think had the most significant impact on American culture?

- Science—Why are scientific demonstrations and experiments important?

- Mathematics—Provide some ways to assess the understanding of your mathematic students. How do you write math?

to a question, be honest with the interviewer and then proceed with a possible response or approach. Mention that you would consult an expert in the field or a practitioner working with this special population or program for further information. At the end of the interview, ask the questions you have prepared for the interviewer.

Coming into an interview with your portfolio sends a message that you are a serious candidate. It also may help to hang on to something—like a metaphorical security blanket—during the interview. If the interviewer doesn't ask to see the portfolio, you decide on the best time to offer it. Many candidates like to present the portfolio after the interviewer asks if the candidate has any questions. It is always good to have a question or two and then lead into opening your portfolio to a section or lesson plan that you want to share. The interviewer should begin to see and hear you as a teacher now and not just a candidate answering the standard job applicant questions.

When the interview is over, ask the interviewer what you can expect to happen next. Inform the interviewer that you will call in a week or two to check on the status of your application.

If the next step is to be interviewed by the school principal, repeat the same preparation process. The preservice teacher may want to compile a miniportfolio to leave with the school principal. The miniportfolio can include copies of "your résumé, a teaching philosophy statement, a classroom management plan (CMP), specific lesson and unit plans, letters of recommendation, and evaluations from field experiences" (Bosch, 2006, p. x). The principal may be interviewing multiple candidates over a few days and when it comes time to review candidates, the miniportfolio may be that extra credential!

You may be asked to conduct your interview over the telephone. AAEE's 2015 ***AAEE Job Search Handbook for Educators*** offers tips—including sample questions to ask and answer—on how to handle a telephone interview.

CHAPTER TWO

What Do I Do First?

I. I'm Hired—What's Next?

You have been notified that you have a job. Take a deep breath and say, "Thank you very much. I'm looking forward to the start of my teaching career."

A first-year teacher described these feelings in a journal entry:

> *I'm hired! She just told me that I'm hired. I couldn't get my breath; my body was shaking, and then out of me came this weak, meek voice that said, "Thank you." When I hung up the phone, I shouted, "I am a teacher for real!" Then came thoughts like "Where do I start? What do I do first? Help! Who can help me?"*

Now, the work begins. You are no longer a student or a job applicant; you are a teacher. Studies of the beginning years of teaching have described the transition from student to teacher as difficult for most first-year teachers (Hoak, 1999; Knowles, 1990; Lovette, 1996; Ryan, 1970; Veenman, 1984). Beginning teaching experiences are important as they influence teachers' practices and attitude throughout their careers (Kuzmic, 1994). To ensure a smooth transition, you need to plan a very good start to your first year.

The following journal entry of a first-year teacher provides some insight into feeling unprepared.

> *My first day, I never felt ready for the kids. I was doing so well before they arrived. I really needed more days without the students to prepare for them. Is this a natural feeling?*

II. Before School Starts

Planning ahead is essential for the first year of teaching. The most valuable time you have is the time between being hired and the opening day of school. New teachers should engage in extensive planning before school starts (Davis, Resta, Miller, & Fortman, 1999; Emmer & Evertson, 2012; Evertson & Emmer, 2012; Hoak, 1999).

Too many first-year teachers wait until the first in-service day to get started, which is only a few days before the doors open for students. These teachers are behind before they have even started. Catching up is difficult for a first-year teacher.

As a first step, count the days you have before reporting to the school. Fill out a schedule or calendar outlining your plan for preparation before school starts. Schedule something each day. More than 200 veteran and first-year teachers offered the following comments on what they have done or wished they had done before the school year started.

Visit the School

A new teacher must visit the school several times prior to the first day of school. The first visit will introduce you to the community, school, and the school's staff. Drive around the area and take a look around. See where the children you'll be teaching live and play. Some schools organize a "Community Walk" during the beginning in-service days prior to school starting. When you visit the school, greet and introduce yourself to everyone. Allow plenty of time to listen and speak with the faculty and staff. Find your assigned room and locate school offices, as well as the cafeteria, library, clinic, gym, audiovisual equipment room, and computer labs. In addition, find the teachers' lounge, vending machines, and copying machine. Before leaving, borrow one or two teachers' magazines found in the lounge or library. Read the publications and copy interesting ideas. The September issues of teaching journals are filled with great ideas for starting school.

On your next visit, attempt to learn some specifics about your school. Ask to see the school policy and faculty handbooks. Inquire about previewing the textbooks and study guides. Read the texts thoroughly and begin to think about ways to teach the topics. Start collecting ideas, materials, and information pertaining to the topics. Having the curriculum in mind will allow you to find relevant materials in newspapers, magazines, and books, as well as identify activities and resources to support the topics. You may want to search for unusual facts, unique activities, and creative ways to introduce lessons and units. On this visit, ask for the following information:

- Ask to see a progress report form and a report card so that you will be aware of the areas of evaluation. Inquire about the grading scale.

- Ask for a class roster and a school photograph of members of your class (class book, pictures in cumulative files) to begin associating names with faces.

- Ask to review the cumulative folders of students in your class to gain information pertaining to students having special learning needs.

- Ask about the specific types of technology and computer software that will be available for administrative and instructional tasks. Ask about the procedures for securing limited resources such as digital cameras, smart boards, and laptops. Ask about the number of computers available in each classroom.

Off to a Good Start

Organizing your classroom is an essential part of the advance preparation that is key to a successful first day, first month, and first year. For most first-year teachers, preparing the room is fun and a way to personalize the surroundings. Research shows that effective teachers create positive learning environments by using management skills to organize time, space, materials, auxiliary personnel, and students (Davis et al., 1999; Hoak, 1999; Lovette, 1996; McDaniel, 1986; Strother, 1985). The first-year teacher can begin by sketching the room and making some decisions about room arrangement. The following suggestions are ways to start creating an attractive and positive learning environment:

- Arrange desks and prepare a seating chart. Begin by identifying a teaching position in the front of the room. Radiate the students' desks from this position in pairs, rows, or groups of four. Consider creating one or two semicircles of desks.

- Create one or two colorful, inviting, and interesting bulletin boards. Reserve a space in the room for the students to create a bulletin board sometime during the first week.

- Establish a culturally responsive classroom environment. Purchase and display in the classroom a map of the world that highlights students' countries of origin. Display a banner that welcomes students in many different languages. Post pictures and posters in the classroom that reflect people of different cultures. Select books for the class library that promote themes of diversity, tolerance, and community, such as **Crow Boy** (Yashima, 1983), **The Sneetches and Other Stories** (Seuss, 1989), **The Crayon Box That Talked** (DeRolf, 1997) and **Chrysanthemum** (Henkes, 1991), as suggested by Weinstein, Curran and Tomlinson-Clark (2003, p. 271).

- Plan one or two age-appropriate learning centers. The custodian may be able to help you find a large table or two and some additional chairs to create a learning center.

- Use the computer in your classroom as part of a learning center. Check the availability of age-appropriate software.

- Set up a class library. Ask the librarian (media specialist) for trade books that are age appropriate, interesting, and exciting for the students.

- Design a reading corner if your room is large enough. This can be done with pillows or carpet squares. An elaborate entry to the reading center, such as a tent or an igloo, might be an interesting possibility.

- Plan a unique way to label your door with your name and room number. It is important to establish an identity.

FIGURE 2.1   *Ideas to Start Off the Year in Elementary School*

1. Check student/parent/guardian phone numbers and addresses against those listed in the cumulative (cum) record.

2. Check to see if the last names are different from their parents. Who has legal custody? Who can pick up the child and who cannot?

3. Check for students that have serious health problems, allergies, and so forth.

4. Check for students who have special needs, go out for special programs, or go to speech therapy, for example.

5. Review the bus schedules and make note cards of information specific to each student, such as who walks, who goes to an after-school program, where the child goes if there is a weather emergency or school is dismissed early.

6. Call the parent or guardian of each student to introduce yourself. The call must be a positive one.

7. Assign coat hooks or cubbies.

8. Set up a homework board so assignments can be copied before going home.

Some additional ideas from veteran teachers are compiled in Figure 2.1.

You may be asking yourself, how can I know for sure how to get a good start to my first school year? Pedota (2007) compiled a list of ten classroom management ideas in an article titled, **"Strategies for Effective Classroom Management in the Secondary Setting"** (p. 165). One of his ideas is to think about "we" rather than "I" in setting up the classroom environment. In thinking about and preparing for your first year, the following thoughts apply to all teachers in all classroom settings:

1. Care about and believe in each student. Provide every one with plenty of opportunities for success.

2. Apply the golden rule—treat students as you would like them to treat you. Model behaviors you want from your students.

3. Establish a class motto, such as "In our class, we will work together, learn together, and succeed together."

4. Provide opportunities for students to apply self-control or self-correct inappropriate behaviors without a consequence.

5. Keep parents or guardians on your side.

6. Laugh out loud many times during the day.

FIGURE 2.2 *Postcard to Students*

Dear Susan,

I am so excited that you are going to be a part of our third-grade class.

   We will be doing a lot of fun things this year. You will learn your multiplication tables and how to write in cursive.

   Please bring a picture of yourself on the first day.

   See you next week.

Student _____

100 Student Road ____

Student, VA 22222 ____

                              Sincerely,
                              Teacher's Name

Below are more helpful suggestions for starting school collected from first-year teachers, second- and third-year teachers, and more experienced teachers (including the authors):

- Send out **postcards** introducing yourself to your students and highlighting the year. See Figure 2.2 for a sample postcard. One elementary teacher reported that she sends out party invitations to her class members inviting them to a "get-together" the first day of school.

- Call **parents or guardians and introduce yourself and share something GOOD** about their child. This will make the parents or guardians feel more comfortable. They may be more responsive to you later if there is a problem to discuss or a request to partner for improvement. Let the students know that you are glad they are in your class. Suggest to parents or guardians that teaching is a shared responsibility, and a partnership leads to much success for the student. Call parents or guardians on three separate evenings, for example, call one-third of the parents or guardians on Tuesday, one-third on Wednesday, and one-third on Thursday, or five a night or five each week.

- Prepare a **file folder for each student** to collect work samples and document certain behaviors. Set up additional file folders with labels such as the following: "Rainy Day File"—teaching ideas, materials, and projects with materials collected in advance; "Fillers File"—work sheets, games, interesting facts, duplicated activities, and ideas for immediate use; "Fun File"—for arts and crafts or experiments requiring materials that are already available in the classroom or collected in advance; "Ideas File"—for ideas clipped from teacher journals and ideas from other teachers; and "Bulletin Board File"—for sketched ideas or ideas clipped from newspapers or journals or from other teachers. You may want to purchase colored file folders for coding purposes.

- Start a **file for substitute teachers** in which you will put a class schedule, class seating chart, daily routines, extra work sheets, and a list of several fun activities and games that your students enjoy. See Figure 2.3 for a sample

FIGURE 2.3 *Sample Class Schedule*

Date _____ Teacher _____ Room _____ Grade _____

Time		
7:30 7:55	Morning Assignments	Sharpen two pencils. Copy homework assignments in composition books. Math: Spelling:
7:55 8:05	SQUIRT	Sustained Quiet Uninterrupted Reading Time—Read a book of your choice silently.
8:05 8:10	Clerical	Collect library books. Say Pledge of Allegiance. Write down absences on absence list. Take lunch count.
8:15 8:45	Science/ Soc. Studies	
8:45 9:15	Music	Walk them to Room _____ (room number), _____ (teacher's name).
9:15 9:30	Bathroom	Line up boys first, then girls. Use the bathrooms in the back hall.
12:00 12:30	Lunch	Table 7. Line up in this order: children who are buying milks and snacks, hot lunches, then children with lunch boxes.
12:35 12:50	Recess	Recess helpers should get the equipment. Go out to the bus ramp. Children may play on the blacktop or on the playground.

class schedule. Check with your principal for the guidelines for the substitute file. Remember to ask other teachers for ideas for this file.

- Make a large, colorful **display of students' names** outside your classroom door. Invite them to begin a new year with you. One first-year teacher suggested placing outlines of tennis shoes (sneakers) on the wall outside the classroom door with each sneaker having a student's name on it. The caption placed above the sneakers could read "Sneaking into Sixth Grade with Ms. Smith." Another first-year teacher used the theme "Happy New Year!" and placed horns, hats, and streamers on the door and a class roster in the middle.

- Make a large **attendance chart that also serves to collect the lunch count.** Laminate a name card for each student and attach a magnet. Student will be able to move their names to the appropriate lunch choice. You will be able to quickly scan the chart for attendance and lunch information.

- Make a large chart or **bulletin board to highlight student jobs** in the classroom. Laminate it and prepare it in a way that allows you to put up new names every week, every two weeks, or monthly.

- Laminate a **chart of the daily and weekly class schedule.** This schedule informs the teacher and students of changes, events, or special classes. A blocked schedule form for distribution to students on a weekly basis may be helpful.

- Make **extra copies of the class roster** and the seating chart. These forms are helpful for the many times you must keep records throughout the school year, for example, recording which students bring in required school forms and homework papers. Create an electronic class roster.

- Create and duplicate a **form that can be attached to students' work** requesting a parent/guardian signature and comments.

- **Ask a veteran teacher** in the school to tell you **what happens on the first day.** Take notes.

- **Purchase a subscription to a teachers' magazine.**

- **Visit a teachers' store** in your area.

- **Review age-appropriate fiction and nonfiction books.** Choose some that you will be able to read aloud to your students. Commit some stories to memory. Become a storyteller!

- Make a **list of required materials** students will need.

- **Shop early** to get your basic school supplies before the stores run out of everything.

A first-year teacher humorously suggested that a teacher supply list should include chalk-colored clothes, comfortable shoes, and a large bottle of aspirin to begin the year. More serious items to purchase prior to the start of school are

- ☐ adhesive notes
- ☐ calendar
- ☐ large canvas tote
- ☐ chart paper
- ☐ colored markers
- ☐ colored paper
- ☐ file folders
- ☐ file trays for paper collection
- ☐ hand lotion
- ☐ index cards
- ☐ letter cutouts
- ☐ antibacterial solution or wipes
- ☐ computer paper

- ☐ masking tape
- ☐ notebook paper
- ☐ paper clips
- ☐ pencils
- ☐ poster board
- ☐ rubber stamp of your name
- ☐ scissors
- ☐ scotch tape
- ☐ two-sided sticky tape
- ☐ dry erase markers
- ☐ timer
- ☐ tissues
- ☐ stapler and staples

In addition to this supply list, you may want to purchase books, a bookcase or other furniture, and a rug or carpet remnant. Garage sales are great places to collect such items inexpensively. Some "dollar" stores are stocked with various classroom supplies, treats, and necessities for the new teacher and will definitely help you stay on a budget.

III. Preparing for the First Day

The first day is like a first impression—it has to be good. In the following journal entries, first-year teachers reflected on that first day.

> Today was the first day of my career, I can't believe it. I felt as if I was in a daze. It was neither a bad day nor a great day. It was just kind of there.

> My first day went like this: I started, stopped, was interrupted by announcements and started again, was stopped again, and was interrupted by a knock at the door. It was time to switch classes. Chaos ensued! Kids leaving every which way for somewhere. Not knowing students' names, I was helpless to prevail!

The thirteen suggestions compiled below can help you plan for a successful first day. You may want to use this listing as a check list:

1. Prepare a letter for parents and guardians outlining goals and objectives for the school year. Distribute the letter at the end of the first day.

2. Plan a unique way to introduce yourself to the class. An example might be to come to school with a large duffle bag. Inside the bag are things that tell the students something about you. The bag could contain the following items: a tennis racket, beach towel, sunglasses, favorite book, picture of a pet, bag of potato chips, and diet soda. The students could prepare and share such a bag the next few days. Not only would it help introduce them to their classmates, but it would help you get to know them better as well.

3. Create an online interest survey for the first day. Check to see if your school has a survey tool available for you to use. Information taken from the survey will help you establish positive relationships with your students and help them build strong peer relationships. It can make your teaching more interesting, relevant, and personal. Continue to survey the students throughout the year and use the information to make assignments, form groups, and plan enrichment activities.

4. Write student names or numbers on Popsicle sticks or tongue depressors. If you use numbers, assign each student a number. Put all the sticks in a jar. Use the sticks to call on students the first few days. This will help you get to know student names quickly. These sticks can be used throughout the school year to call on people, assign jobs, and line up the students randomly.

5. Prepare some review sheets (not lengthy) from the first few chapters of the subject matter texts. Children enjoy maps, graphic organizers, word puzzles, and games. The information gained from the activities is invaluable for assessing students' knowledge and planning how much time to spend on review. Websites such as **www.puzzlemaker.com** can provide many great ideas.

6. Plan the spelling lesson and activities for the first week. Try to use words that are associated with other subject areas as well.

7. Plan some student work to be completed on the first day. Write a positive comment or two on each completed assignment. Pass out the work at the end of the day with other items to take home.

8. Outline and teach a few procedures that will be necessary for the first day: use of bathroom passes, sharpening pencils, taking attendance, turning in class work.

9. Think about the cue you would like to use in your classroom to gain students' attention: a whistle, a clap, lights, a raised hand, a signal, or your moving to the center of the room. Teach the cue and begin using it the first day.

10. Take each student's picture using a digital camera. Then place a magnetic strip on the backs of the pictures and place them on the board. Each morning, when your students come in, have them take their pictures down and place in a bin. This is another quick way of viewing attendance. You can use the pictures in other assignments and activities throughout the year.

11. Begin weekly folders for all graded papers on the first day. Have students personalize the folders. Prepare short forms to include in the folders that describe homework currently assigned or missing, behavior checklists to indicate level of progress, work habits noted as satisfactory or needed, and a place for parent or guardian and student signatures, along with teacher comments. In addition to being time-savers, the folder and forms are great communication tools when sending work home, noting areas of progress or needing support, and providing documentation when conferencing with a parent or guardian or student.

12. Assign some class jobs to begin the second day of class.

13. Distribute "Great Moments" form to your students to take home the first day. Create a nicely decorated form using a computer template. Personalize each form with a child's name, and fill in the child's observable great behavior moment.

    (Write child's name) had a GREAT MOMENT today. He offered to help his friend, Timmy, get caught up on his assignments. (Timmy had been sick and had gotten behind in his work.)

The computer is a great resource for creating many items needed in a classroom. You can use a variety of software applications to create materials for your classroom. You can enlarge pages for display by printing single documents at 400 percent and tape or glue along the lines to create a poster if your school doesn't have a digital poster printer. You can create name tags for students, print file folder labels using special label paper, generate station labels for learning centers, and many other such ideas. Remember to use photographs, clip art, and word art to enhance the document and be sure to cite all sources appropriately or check for copyright clearance if necessary.

IV. Survival Advice

Yes, the first day will end. A first-year teacher wrote, "With every new experience, good or indifferent, remember, this too will pass." You may be wondering how students see first-year teachers. Interviews were conducted (Bosch, 1991) with twenty-five sixth-grade students in a large, urban school. The majority of these sixth-graders reported that they could identify first-year teachers by the following characteristics: inconsistent, lenient, nervous, slow to handle discipline problems, want to be your friend, and they have evaluators in their rooms all the time. When asked if students are hard on first-year teachers, they responded unanimously, "Yes." Students agreed that the phrase they say most often to inexperienced teachers is "But, my last year's teachers didn't do it that way." When asked if they had some advice for first-year teachers, several students said that they should handle discipline problems faster and never pick favorites.

Interviews were conducted by Bosch again in 2010 with twenty sixth-graders and the students' responses were basically the same. Of interest to note, one response about having evaluators in their rooms all of the time was not mentioned. All interviewed students still agreed that they were hard on first-year teachers. In terms of the advice they would offer to first-year teachers, one additional suggestion was expressed and that was for first-year teachers to be consistent, and as one student put it, share their bottom line with us.

What advice do surveyed teachers have for surviving the first year? When well over one hundred practicing teachers were asked, their advice was as follows:

- Get to know the school custodian and the secretary well. They know what is going on in school.

- Be able to say no to committee involvement or extracurricular assignments. Use the reply "My first year of teaching is enough for me to concentrate on at the moment, but ask me again."

- Refrain from correcting papers or writing lesson plans at faculty meetings.

- Try not to complain, as misery finds too much company.

- Begin class as soon as the bell rings.

- Plan activities for students who finish their work before others.

- Anticipate the behavior of children before and after holidays and long weekends, on field trips, and when evaluators come into the room. Some teachers mentioned that student behavior changes on rainy days.

- Decide what kind of homework to assign and how much. Check with the school principal for the homework policy.

- Keep your e-mail accounts separate. Use your professional (school) e-mail account only for business and school-related activities. Maintain an external e-mail account (AOL, Yahoo, MSN, or your home internet provider) for personal matters.

- Never give out your home phone number.

- Give yourself a break! Be easy on yourself.

- Try not to give up!

It has been said that teaching is the only profession where the beginner is expected to do what the veteran does and with equal success (Davis et al., 1999; Tonnsen &

Patterson, 1992; Worthy, 2005). As one new teacher wrote in her journal, "I wish we came with a set of directions."

Principal Joanne Rooney (2004, p. 86) writes that she visits every primary classroom and shares with the students that "learning is all that counts." She tells this story each year:

> *While walking on a Lake Michigan beach one summer, I spotted a little boy, about five years old, in bright blue swimming trunks. He was running back and forth, filling a large yellow bucket with water from the lake, hurrying to dump the water in a big hole in the sand, and then repeating the process. I asked what he was doing, "Oh," he said, "I plan to empty the whole lake into the hole I've dug, and it might take me all day so I must hurry." And with that, he returned to the endless task.*

Rooney continues by explaining to the children that "there is a whole lake of things for them to learn and they must work very hard to empty as much of that lake of knowledge into their brains as possible." She laughs because later when she asked the children about the little boy on the beach, many have missed the message but seem to recall the color of the boy's swimsuit or bucket, for example; but the teachers get the message that "learning should be the sole benchmark for all school decisions" (p. 87).

CHAPTER THREE

How Do I Prepare for Co-Teaching?

I. I'm Hired for an Inclusive Classroom—Now What?

Scenario: First-Year Special Education Teacher in an Inclusive Classroom

You have been hired to teach in an inclusive classroom. The word *co-teaching* was mentioned. Many first-year teachers have had little student teaching experience working in an inclusive classroom.

This journal entry depicts the confusion over the roles the two teachers have in a co-teaching learning environment.

A first-year special education teacher writes in her journal that

> *Sometimes it seemed like I was the only one who didn't know what was going on or should be happening. I can say that the teacher I was assigned to co-teach with was very welcoming and instantly informed me of my responsibilities in her classroom: she was the content teacher and would deliver all of the instruction while I, as the special educator, was to circulate and monitor, clarify, and keep students on task. It sounded to me that I was in a subservient role but I had a job.*

Another special education teacher writes in his journal about feeling unprepared for an inclusive classroom:

> *How can you be prepared for the unexpected situations that continue to happen in an inclusive classroom? I guess you can say that your first year is a "live and learn" experience.*

II. Understanding an Inclusive Classroom

The Individuals with Disabilities Education Act (IDEA) of 2004 requires educating students in their least restrictive environment (LRE). For students with disabilities, placement in their least restrictive environment enhances the achievement of individualized educational plan (IEP) objectives, the development of social and communication skills, and the generalization of skills. In order to promote success for students with disabilities in general education settings, general and special educators need to work together. An inclusive classroom is recognized as a learning environment where a general education teacher is paired with a special education teacher and both teachers have the responsibility to meet the needs of all learners in the classroom.

Halvorsen and Neary (2001) explain that an inclusive classroom is where students with disabilities are supported in chronologically age-appropriate general education classes in their home schools. They receive the specialized instruction outlined by their IEPs within the context of the core curriculum and general class activities. According to Cushman (2004) and Shumway, Gallo, Dickson, and Gibbs (2011), co-teaching is a shared situation where two people engage in the role of teaching and share the responsibility and accountability for student learning.

There are several models of co-teaching. One model is the One Teach, One Observe model. In this model, one teacher is the primary instructor, while the other teacher collects data, reviews the material, and determines learning outcomes of the students. Another model is referred to as the One Teach, One Drift model. This model is defined as one teacher being the primary instructor, while the other teacher monitors student work and behavior. It is important to note that in both models either teacher can take the lead role. In the literature, these models are not considered the most effective methods of co-teaching, but they have specific benefits.

A third model is Parallel Teaching, which allows each teacher to teach the material to half of the students independently. Parallel Teaching reduces the student-to-teacher ratio. It is important in a co-teaching classroom environment to vary the groups of students, and the teachers should teach both groups. It has been suggested that using this model can provide the opportunities to match the student's learning style with a specific teacher's teaching style.

Station Teaching is another co-teaching model. The teachers divide students and content into two areas called stations in the classroom and each teacher is responsible for delivering half of the content in each station. The students rotate from one station to another independently or in groups. The content in the stations should be independent of each other, not built upon each other, because the order of the stations for the students will vary. It is also important to vary the grouping of the students in Station Teaching.

Another co-teaching model, Alternative or Supplemental Model, is when two teachers in the same classroom teach the same information using two different teaching styles. The group sizes may vary and student placement within groups may change. This model is very conducive to reteaching material or adding rigor for higher-achieving students.

All of the models have their strengths and weaknesses and specific situations where they are appropriate. It is significant to note that co-teaching implies that both teachers are actively involved in teaching. There is no leader of the classroom, but rather the teachers share the responsibility of the classroom instruction and management. The teachers are working together, bouncing ideas off of each other, and providing smooth transitions between topics. The teachers are a tag team in the classroom creating a positive environment for learning.

Co-Teaching in an Inclusive Classroom

Let's examine further the word *co-teaching*. Sileo (2005) defines co-teaching as an instructional delivery approach in which general and special educators share responsibility for planning, delivery, and evaluation of instructional techniques to heterogeneous groups of students in an integrated setting.

The definition of co-teaching in an inclusive classroom has been loosely defined and interpreted in schools and can appear very differently in implementation. In general, co-teaching in an inclusive classroom is not described as team teaching. Team teaching is typically two general education teachers working together in a classroom. It also refers to the planning of content, not the delivery of content. Inclusion suggests a philosophy of student involvement in a classroom setting rather than a teaching method. In the ideal co-teaching classroom environment in an inclusive classroom, it is important to understand that collaboration is an activity, not a teaching method.

Forming a Co-Teaching Partnership

Co-teaching is a partnership that requires careful planning for teaching and reaching all learners. It takes dedication in developing a co-teaching partnership and perseverance in sustaining a positive working relationship in the classroom. In an ideal co-teaching classroom environment it is impossible to identify which teacher is the general education teacher and which is the special education teacher. The students should view the teachers as equal partners with student success as a priority.

The following steps support this collaborative activity: working together, planning instruction together, co-teaching planned instruction, and evaluating student learning outcomes together. This means the teachers must take time to work together to create and plan the lessons in order to effectively present the lessons. It is imperative to have administrative support for the co-teaching setting. An example would be a shared time during the day for partners to plan or reflect on co-taught lessons.

The first step in forming a co-teaching partnership in an inclusive classroom begins with a commitment to shared responsibility for the learning of both general education and special education students. It is important to discuss teaching philosophies. Together, the teachers must develop a teaching philosophy for an inclusive classroom and for working together. It is essential for the two parties to have a shared belief or vision regarding co-teaching. This philosophy will encourage teamwork and ensure shared responsibility for the learning of all students in the classroom. Additionally, it will help minimize misunderstandings and motivate a healthy problem-solving environment, which can abate controversy or problems.

Next, the teachers need to decide on the co-teaching role each teacher has in this inclusive classroom learning environment. Forming a positive co-teaching partnership in an inclusive classroom is to clarify the role each teacher has in teaching and make a commitment to the purpose of working together in this classroom environment. Even though each teacher approaches the classroom from different roles, each teacher must realize the student learning needs are addressed together. Murawski and Dieker (2008) have repeatedly reminded teachers working in a co-teaching classroom environment that the service delivery options designed to address the needs of general and special education students need to be addressed by both teachers. The general and special education teachers should define their roles in an inclusive classroom before the students arrive.

Together, the teachers need to establish ways to co-manage the learning environment. The classroom tasks and responsibilities are to be clearly defined for each teacher. Determining how the classroom works is based on mutually agreed upon decisions. The teachers develop classroom rules, procedures, incentives, and consequences. Each teacher needs to respond to classroom issues in the same manner to provide the students with consistency. It is helpful if the co-teachers discuss some "what-if" situations in establishing and maintaining a positive learning environment for co-teaching.

Co-teaching and inclusive programs have their challenges. It is also imperative to recognize that things will go wrong, especially in the beginning. Just like any partnership, it takes time to develop. In these situations, the teachers must support each other and together work through challenges and difficulties. Co-teaching is an evolving partnership that will take time. Each year working together will solidify the partnership and enhance the relationship between the teachers, ultimately leading to a more successful learning environment.

Be Proactive

A proactive way to prepare for a successful co-teaching partnership is to promote a dialogue between the general and special education teacher. The Co-Teaching Compatibility Inventory (CCI) is designed to establish a collaborative dialogue that results in co-teachers getting to know each other personally and professionally. The Co-teaching Compatibility Inventory consists of ten questions. After each co-teacher independently completes the ten questions under the personal response section 1, the teachers plan a time to get together and share their responses to the questions. The responses to the questions begin the dialogue needed to form a successful co-teaching relationship. After discussing the personal responses to the questions together, both teachers should collaborate to create mutually agreed-upon responses to the ten questions in section 2 of the CCI. The mutually agreed-upon responses to the ten questions can be revisited, revised, and edited for more specificity or clarity. The continual focus on the mutually agreed-upon responses embody the foundation for a successful co-teaching partnership.

Co-Teaching Compatibility Inventory (CCI)

Co-teaching questions	*Section 1: Creating a personal response to the questions*	*Section 2: Creating a mutual response to the questions*
1. How do I define co-teaching?		
2. How do I define co-teaching in an inclusive classroom?		
3. What do I see as the role of the general education teacher?		
4. What do I see as the role of the special education teacher?		
5. What do I see as my role in co-teaching?		
6. What do I see as the best way to work together in an inclusive classroom?		
7. What are my student behavioral expectations in a shared classroom?		
8. What personal skills do I bring to the collaborative partnership?		
9. What professional skills do I bring to the collaborative partnership?		
10. What are my plans for reflecting on our co-teaching partnership for improvement?		

CHAPTER FOUR

How Do I Work With Parents or Guardians?

I. Parent or Guardian Involvement

Studies have reported that parental involvement is beneficial to students' academic success (Epstein, 1994; Hiatt-Michael, 2001). Henderson (1987) states students do better in school when their parents or guardians are involved in their education. In the study of American high schools, James Coleman reasons that the single outstanding characteristic common to those private and parochial schools that outperformed many public high schools was that they had a different relationship to their community. Coleman surmises that private schools and parochial schools "see themselves as extensions of the families they serve" (Henderson, 1987, p. 8).

When children are aware that their teachers and parents or guardians know each other, work together for common goals, form meaningful relationships on their behalf, and share mutual ownership for their school success, they may accept the responsibility necessary to work to their potential. In other words, when there is a continuous flow of communication between home and school, the child's educational experience is greatly enhanced.

Findings from the research conducted by the National Parent Teacher Association (PTA) reveal that

> *when parents are involved in their child's education, the child does better academically, regardless of the socioeconomic status or ethnic/cultural background of the family, regardless of the age of the child. Not only that, but there is increased likelihood of the child displaying cooperative behavior, positive attitudes, and completing and submitting homework on time. With parental involvement, students are more likely to have regular attendance, to graduate, and to go on to some form of post-secondary education. (E. Kottler, J. A. Kottler, & C. J. Kottler, 2004, p. 118)*

Many parents or guardians are reluctant to get involved in the classroom. In an effort to alert parents or guardians to their value in the classroom—beyond the usual clerical tasks, providers of classroom parties, and chaperones for field trips—the administration of the University of California-Los Angeles (UCLA) laboratory school (Hunter, 1989) identified three possible categories of competencies:

1. Skills in hobbies and crafts

2. Direct knowledge and experience in occupations

3. Appreciation of, knowledge of, or skills in many aspects of different cultures

The UCLA administrators invited parents and guardians to a two-hour in-service session, where teachers demonstrated effective teaching techniques and illustrated ways to make lessons successful. Care was also taken to help parents and guardians develop a sensitivity to issues of privacy and confidentiality so that they would adopt professional precautions to protect children and their families. The results were over-whelmingly successful. The parents and guardians who participated in this process were more willing to take active roles in their children's education, and the teachers reported improvement in their children's academic performance.

Jennings (1989) found most parents and guardians have the ability, energy, and talent to play all roles at school, including that of decision maker. In those schools where parents and guardians are invited to become involved in higher-level deci-sions, there is more creativity, resourcefulness, and ingenuity displayed. In fact, when parents and guardians are challenged to contribute their energy and ideas, significant changes are made toward educational progress and resource allocations. Furthermore, the more parents and guardians are represented at the decision-making table, the less finger-pointing and blaming occurs, and the more shared responsibility and respect are modeled in the community. Ribas (1998, p. 83) reminds teachers that "in many schools, the new generation of parents is older, busier, better educated, and more assertive, acting as consumers of their chil-dren's education." Bill Simmer, a parent-relations consultant, sees a shift over the past three decades regarding how parents view schools. He explains, "Parents are approaching schools with much more of a contract mentality. . . . Expecting results from schools has come well within the realm of parenting" (Keller, 2008, p. 2).

Children of all ages need to have their parents or guardians take an active interest in their schooling. It is easy for parents or guardians to underestimate their importance to their children. Often when children become adolescents, parents or guardians feel they should back off, for fear their children will think they are overbearing or their children's teachers will think they are overprotective. Actually, teenagers need their parents or guardians to stay involved with their teachers and in school activities. Although outwardly they may seem nonchalant or callous, inwardly they very much need caring parents or guardians who will help them as they navigate the frightening seas to adulthood (Berla, 1992; Compton-Lilly, 1999; Gould, 1999; Patterson, Baldwin, Gonzales, Guadarrams, & Keith, 1999; Shockley, Michalove, &

Allen, 1995; Sleeter & Grant, 2008). Therefore, it is absolutely essential that parents or guardians and teachers sign up on the same team with the child. If either pulls against the other, undermines the other, belittles or criticizes the other, the effect will be lower performance on the part of the child.

If the benefit of working together is so obvious, why is it so difficult to achieve? Some of the answer lies in our history. Some teachers and parents or guardians recall bad experiences from the past that consciously or unconsciously affect their present working relationships. More of the answer may result from feelings of inadequacy from both the teacher and parent or guardians. It's human nature to shy away from encounters that may become confrontational or unpleasant or in which we may be put on the defensive. Some parents or guardians, specifically, see themselves as advocates for their children in competitive times (Keller, 2008). In many well-to-do school districts, demanding adults have made teachers' jobs harder. The answer to forming a positive and productive working relationship is to focus on the child. Everyone—teacher, parent or guardian, and child—must commit to working together for more school success.

Listed below are many of the reported obstacles to parent or guardian involvement— possible reasons why parents or guardians and teachers may feel uncomfortable working together. When teachers and parents or guardians can see that both parties feel vulnerable—and at times unsure and anxious—each will be willing to put forth the extra effort it takes to WORK TOGETHER on behalf of the child.

Teacher Fears About Parents or Guardians

Teachers are unsure of the role parents or guardians want to play in the classroom. In workshops I have conducted, many teachers have had concerns about the parents' or guardians' motives; others have felt hopeless, expressing their concern that the dynamics between the two groups would always be suspicious of the other. It may be helpful to view responses made by veteran teachers about parents or guardians in order to truly understand the dynamics of parent or guardian involvement in schools. Below are lists of the fears that teachers have expressed about parents or guardians.

- Parents or guardians may want to spend too much volunteer time in their child's class, which may create problems for the child or teacher.

- Parents' or guardians' presence may cause behavior problems with their child.

- Children may be embarrassed or uncomfortable about their parents' or guardians' involvement in the class.

- Parents or guardians may be excessively harsh with their own child or with other students.

- Parents or guardians may show favoritism, focused only on their own child, or on the other hand, may ignore their child, overcompensating in an effort to be fair.

- Parents or guardians may try to handle discipline problems themselves instead of consulting the teacher.

- The teacher and the parent or guardian may both feel uncertain as to who should discipline if the parent or guardian's child misbehaves.

- The teacher may feel pressured to give special consideration to the parent or guardian's child while the parent or guardian is in the classroom.

- A parent or guardian may take too much responsibility in the class without checking with the teacher first.

- A parent or guardian may become "over involved," always dropping in unexpectedly or demanding too much of the teacher's time.

- Teachers may feel that they will be unable to rely on parents or guardians to show up when scheduled.

- A parent or guardian may lack the skills necessary to work with children.

- A parent or guardian may give incorrect information when tutoring.

- A parent or guardian may make judgments about a teacher's ability to handle the class.

- A parent or guardian may break the confidentiality of the classroom by talking to other parents about a particular child's behavior or situation.

- Parents or guardians might create problems with other parents or guardians if they criticizes the teacher's methods to them.

- A parent or guardian may be a poor role model.

- The teacher may lack the patience to train the parent or guardian or may be reluctant to do the extra planning required to keep the parent or guardian involved.

- The teacher may feel apprehensive because of a previous experience with another parent or guardian.

- The teacher may have little support if the principal or other members of the school administration feel negatively about parental involvement.

- The teacher may worry that by accepting the parents' guardians' assistance, it will appear that he or she is unable to do the job.

Parent or Guardian Fears About Teachers

Parents or guardians may feel uneasy about speaking with teachers and spending time in the classroom. The following issues are real fears felt by many parents or guardians, as evidenced in workshops for parents (Kersey, 1990/1994), and they must be considered when reaching out to parents or guardians.

- Parents or guardians may fear the teacher will be unwilling to listen to their ideas and concerns.

- Parents or guardians may fear the teacher will judge them or label them as *bad parents*.

- Parents or guardians may fear the teacher will blame them for their child's behavior in school.

- Parents or guardians may not want to hear that their child is having problems, fearing they will be powerless to change whatever is causing the problem.

- Parents or guardians may feel guilty that they didn't take time to help their child.

- Parents or guardians may make false assumptions about the teacher based on what their child has told them.

- Parents or guardians may fear that if they are too assertive the teacher may not like them and take it out on their child.

- Parents or guardians may fear the teacher will compare their child negatively to other children.

- Parents or guardians may fear the teacher will gossip about them or their child to other teachers.

- Parents or guardians may feel as if the teacher is taking over the parental role and they may feel threatened.

- Parents or guardians may fear teachers due to their own negative experiences in school.

- Parents or guardians may fear the unknown of the school system and procedures.

- Parents or guardians may be intimidated by the terminology the teacher uses.

- Parents or guardians may feel intimidated by socioeconomic differences between themselves and the teacher.

- Parents or guardians may feel inferior because of the teacher's degrees.

- Parents or guardians may feel the teacher is merely doing a job and has no real concern for their child.

- Parents or guardians may fear they will be misunderstood or not listened to by the teacher.

- Parents or guardians may feel the school system does not understand their needs or those of their child.

- Parents or guardians may have had learning problems themselves and be embarrassed if their child does, too.

- Parents or guardians may fear exposing too much about the home situation or their own personality.

- Parents or guardians may feel the teacher knows more about them than they want him or her to know.

- Parents or guardians may have much of their self-esteem invested in their child's success and therefore wish to avoid the teacher if there is a chance the teacher may tell them something negative about their child.

II. Effective Communication

The best time for parents or guardians and teachers to get to know each other is before problems arise.

Parents or guardians and teachers have unique, yet overlapping, roles. A parent or guardian's role is to love their child so that the child feels validated as a member of the family and as an individual. The teacher's role is to teach all the children in the class while being aware of their individual needs and differences.

A teacher needs to develop strong and positive communication skills. *Communication* is defined as the verbal or nonverbal exchange of information, meaning, and feelings between two persons. No matter how well prepared the teacher is, no matter how experienced or well trained, if that teacher cannot communicate effectively, he or she will not be successful in the classroom. Parents or guardians need to feel that their concerns are important to teachers. When they feel heard, they will be more enthusiastic about trusting the teacher and the school and more willing to be involved with their child's education.

Developing skills in mirroring and validating communication exchanges seem to hold great promise and relevancy in speaking with parents or guardians. **Mirroring** is the process of accurately reflecting back the contents of a message. The most common form of Co-Teaching Compatibility Inventory (CCI) mirroring is paraphrasing. *Paraphrasing* is summarizing the communication exchange and sending new words back to the sender to make sure each person—sender and receiver—understands the other.

Validation is sending a message to the sender that the information you received makes sense. Validation is a temporary suspension or transcendence of your point of view and allows the other person's experience to have its own reality. Typical validating phrases are "I can see that . . ." or "It makes sense to me that you would think that . . ." or "I can understand that . . . ." The process of mirroring and validation affirms the other person's point of view and fosters a willingness to work together.

Effective communication is essential as it gives the parent or guardian and teacher a working relationship that has meaning. According to Covey (2004), next to physical survival, the greatest need of a human being is psychological survival—to be understood, to be affirmed, and to be validated. Stevens and Tollafield (2003, pp. 523–524) suggest that teachers "monitor their use of communication skills, including reflection, paraphrasing, and summarizing." The authors continue by offering some of the following questions teachers need to ask themselves to know if they are practicing good communication skills:

- Are you making eye contact with the parents or guardians? Are you truly listening to what is being said?

- Is there actual communication and interaction? Is your language easily understandable?

- Are you ready to explain specialized terms such as *standard scores* or *percentile*?

- Has an alliance been formed?

Ribas (1992, pp. 19–20) offers several practical techniques that teachers can use to improve communication with parents or guardians:

- Be a good listener.

- Be positive.

- Be careful how you phrase negative information.

- Be prepared.

- Be sensitive to parents' or guardians' problems.

- Be knowledgeable about the child as a person.

Further, Ribas suggests that teachers call parents or guardians frequently, meet parents or guardians regularly, offer evening conference times, and establish regular office or call-in hours. Time spent planning presentations that leave parents or guardians feeling positive about the school year and not doubting their child's success is very important (Ribas, 1998). There are many formal and informal opportunities for communicating with parents or guardians and planning presentation. Three of the most popular forums for such encounters are the back-to-school event, the open house, and parent -or-guardian-teacher conferences.

III. Back-to-School Event

The back-to-school event is scheduled at the beginning of the school year. Sometimes, this event is scheduled before school actually starts. The parents or guardians and students are usually invited to meet the teacher. This may be a first impression so it must be a positive one. Nelson and Bailey (2008) suggest the teacher should plan to set the tone for the entire year at this event. Henderson, Mapp, Johnson, and Davies (2007, p. 88) provide a six-step agenda for a back-to-school event. The six steps involve asking parents or guardians to talk about their favorite teachers, talking about why you became a teacher, sharing your vision of teaching, discussing how you will help students who are struggling, demonstrating a minilesson, and explaining how to stay in touch with each other.

Not all schools host back-to-school events. In some instances, parents or guardians and children drop by the school on the in-service or work days prior to school starting to introduce themselves. This initial, first-time meeting is important to parents or guardians and to your students.

IV. The Open House

An open house is another opportunity for making a positive first impression. An open house may be the first or second opportunity to meet many of your students' parents or guardians. In **The Teacher's Guide to Success** by Kronowitz (2012, pp. 418–419), ten ideas for a successful open house are discussed. Some of the ideas Kronowitz mentions are providing refreshments, making name tags for parents and guardians, and displaying textbooks. Experienced teachers at your school can also give you valuable advice and help you organize this event. It is wise and useful to get the students involved. Be sure to welcome parents or guardians and encourage them to get involved with their child's class and school. Below are seven suggestions from veteran teachers for planning your first open house.

Planning an Open House

1. Send notes home well in advance to remind everyone of the upcoming open house.

2. Plan an interesting way to introduce yourself to the parents and guardians.

3. Plan to have students' work on display and decorate the room.

4. Prepare a folder of the students' work to be placed on the desks. Allow the parents or guardians to take the folder home.

5. Have a Guest Book for visitors to sign.

6. Plan forms for obtaining volunteers for class projects.

7. Encourage the parents or guardians to write a letter to their son or daughter and leave it on their child's desk.

You may want to design a PowerPoint presentation to cover the main ideas you want to share with parents and guardians. Allow the slides to guide your talk but don't read the slides to the parents and guardians. Keep the contents brief and in bullet form but use clip art, quotes, and some actual pictures of the class. This will ensure that you cover the information and keep everyone focused on what you have to say.

Begin the open house by introducing yourself to the parents and guardians; next, provide a general overview of what the students will be learning this school year and how the class works—the classroom rules, homework policy, grading system, and discipline plan. Next, distribute volunteer sign-up sheets. Conclude with a time for questions. Your principal may announce over the intercom when the open house is over. Some parents or guardians will want to discuss their child individually. Be prepared to say something positive. If anyone wants to schedule a conference, suggest they indicate a convenient time on the appointment sheet located on the table.

Here are some additional ideas to consider in planning and conducting the open house:

- Have the children make invitations to the open house.

- Video-record a message from each member of your class to his or her parent or guardian. When the parents or guardians watch the video, they will understand why it was so important to their child that they come—so they could see their son or daughter on video.

OR

- The teacher might prepare a video depicting the school day to be shown to the parents or guardians. This is a project in which the students would be recorded involved in the various activities of the day, including academic subjects as well as special activities, lunch, and getting on and off the bus.

- This is an excellent way for parents or guardians to learn what an average day is like for their children. (This also lets the teacher off the hook as far as having to stand in front of parents or guardians the whole night.)

- Record the children doing a class activity and use that clip to begin the open house.

- Get the children to make life-size models of themselves and place them at their desks for the open house. They can bring clothes from home, stuff them with paper and attach a paper plate head and feet with features and other details drawn by the student. Parents or guardians love finding their child in the classroom and immediately know where they sit. They can take the life-size model home for the family to enjoy.

OR

- Ask the students to bring in an old T-shirt that they will turn into a puppet representing them. The head can be made from a paper plate and the arms from construction paper. With a coat hanger inside the shirt, the puppet can be attached to the student's chair to greet the parents or guardians. The shirt, with head and hands attached, can also be slipped over the back of the chair. Some "students'" hands could be raised and the children's new work placed on the desks.

- Use an overhead projector to cast shadow and make silhouettes of the children on black paper and place them on the desks. Let the parents or guardians locate their child. The silhouettes make nice keepsakes.

- Have the children leave notes on their desks for their parents or guardians along with a sheet of paper for their parents or guardians to write a response or note.

- Ask the children to finish these sentences about their family:

  My parent or guardian laughs when . . .

  My family's favorite thing to do is . . .

  It makes me happy when my parent or guardian . . .

  I like to help my family . . .

  I like to do _____ with my family . . .

Have the students place these sentences on their desks for their parents or guardians to read and enjoy.

- Using the song "My Favorite Things" from *The Sound of Music*, children can write a list of their favorite things. The children write their names on the back of the list. Hang the lists around the room and have the parents or guardians try to identify their child's list.

- Bring a squish ball to open house. When it is time for introductions, tell one thing about yourself. Then throw the ball to a parent or guardian and ask him or her to do the same, adding the name of his or her child. The ball is thrown to another parent or guardian, who repeats this process. Do this until everyone in the room has been introduced.

V. The Parent-or-Guardian-Teacher Conference

A parent-or-guardian-teacher conference is another opportunity to involve parents or guardians in their children's education. Stevens and Tollafield (2003, p. 521) state that "parent conferences should be models of good communication, integrally involving parents in their child's education." Duplicate and prepare for distribution Figures 4.1, 4.2, 4.3, and 4.4 when planning the parent-or-guardian-teacher conference. Both Kronowitz (2012, pp. 422–423) and Henderson et al. (2007, pp. 293–294) provide checklists to help you have a successful conference. The checklist categories incorporate ideas for what to do before, during, and after the conference.

Planning a Parent-or-Guardian-Teacher Conference

Student portfolios, collections of students' work such as papers, projects, and assignments, are widely used in parent-or-guardian-teacher conferences and are especially useful in the middle and high schools. In the portfolios, the teacher may want to include a project on a country, its geography, and culture, for example, which can serve to connect families of different cultures to the school and classroom.

FIGURE 4.1 *Parent or Guardian Involvement Letter*

Dear Parents or Guardians:

I'm writing to ask you to help me become a partner with you in your child's education. I know my teaching begins with making your child feel at home in my classroom and with helping all the children come together in a learning community. Please help me get to know your child better by completing the following questions. Thank you for your time and sharing your thoughts about your son or daughter.

Sincerely,
Teacher's Name

Your child's name _____

What are your child's strengths? _____

What do you feel is important for me to know about your child? _____

_____

What does your child enjoy doing? _____

Other comments _____

_____

Your name _____ Date _____

Here are six steps to follow in planning a parent-or-guardian-teacher conference:

1. Send a conference letter or form to the parents or guardians with a suggested time. Include spaces for them to acknowledge or suggest a better time to meet. Schedule conferences carefully. Try not to schedule too many conferences in one day and allow break times. Mark those breaks on your conference calendar so you can be on time for each meeting. To keep from being rushed, plan a few conferences a week before and others the week after the official parent conference time. Include some times for working parents or guardians to attend.

2. Confirm the time.

3. Prepare a folder or portfolio for each child containing samples of the student's work.

4. Plan an agenda for discussion.

5. Copy the conference schedule time (form) and jot down items to discuss.

6. Begin and end on a positive note.

FIGURE 4.2   *Sample Parent or Guardian Survey*

Parent or Guardian Survey

Please complete this survey about your child and his or her interests. It will help me to become familiar with your child and assist with his or her needs.

First _____ Middle _____ Last _____

Nickname _____

Address _____

Telephone _____

Birth Date _____

Allergies_____

Your child's favorite things to do _____

_____

_____

Your child's least favorite things to do _____

_____

_____

Things you would like to see your child achieve in school this year _____

_____

_____

Ways you would like to contribute to our class or our school this year (e.g., reading books aloud to the class, computer tutoring, sharing cultural ideas, discussing what you do in your job) _____

_____

_____

FIGURE 4.3 *Sample Form for Parent or Guardian Conference Notes*

Parent or Guardian Conference Notes

Student: _____

Date: _____

Attended by: _____

Items we discussed:_____

Concerns I have: _____

Concerns you have: _____

Strategies I am going to try: _____

Strategies you are going to try: _____

Evaluation of conference: _____

Signed by:

Teacher _____

Student _____

Parent or Guardian _____

FIGURE 4.4 *Sample Form for Parent or Guardian Conference Evaluation*

Parent or Guardian Conference Evaluation

Would you please take a moment to evaluate our conference? Please review the rating scale and answer the questions by circling a number.

The Rating Scale	Excellent		Average		Poor
1. Rate the conference	5	4	3	2	1
2. Was the conference helpful?	5	4	3	2	1
3. Rate the level of information	5	4	3	2	1

If you have any suggestions or comments, please share them with me.

In conducting a conference, begin by arranging a waiting area in the hall with a few adult chairs for early arrivals. Post a daily conference schedule on the door and try to keep to the schedule. Conduct conferences at a table in the back of the room away from the door and not at the teacher's desk. Keep notepaper and pencils handy so that both you and the parents or guardians will be able to keep notes on the conference. It is a good idea to have a box of tissues nearby. Remember to start the conference with a friendly greeting. You may want to begin by sharing one positive experience, remark, or observation pertaining to their child. Provide information in a straightforward and honest manner. Limit the information for discussion and focus on one or two important issues. Be a listener and avoid interruptions. Be mindful of providing specifics and not generalities. During the conference, respond in a precise and positive manner and provide some suggestions for parents or guardians to help them work with their child (see Figure 4.5 on creating an appropriate handout on building a child's self-esteem). Be sure to document the conference. At the end of the conference, walk the parent or guardian to the door before inviting the next parent or guardian to come in.

Some ethical considerations for the conducting the parent-or-guardian-teacher conference are to keep the conference information confidential; avoid comparisons (e.g., this class with other classes or one student with other students or a student with sib-

---

FIGURE 4.5   *Ideas for Parents or Guardians in Building a Child's Self-Esteem*

Elementary Age Specific

1. Show your children that you enjoy them by smiling at them, hugging them, and speaking to them in a positive way.

2. Read out loud together as a family.

3. Take your child with you on trips to run errands and involve him or her in some of the decision making (e.g., "Where should we go first, Grandmother's house or the grocery store?")

4. Take time from work to visit your child's school or eat lunch with him or her.

Middle or Secondary Age Specific

5. Help them discover their own special gifts by letting them develop an interest in activities such as sports, music, and dance.

6. Encourage their independence.

7. Use a democratic form of discipline. Children should be allowed to speak and parents or guardians should listen to what they have to say.

All Age Groups and Grade Levels

8. Use positive reinforcement to encourage responsible behavior.

9. Help them to learn responsibility by requiring them to complete tasks.

10. Set aside a time each day to spend with each child individually.

11. Help children to develop organizational skills by providing space for toys, books, and backpacks and a place to work and study.

12. Get to know their teachers.

13. Do not embarrass your children by yelling at them in public.

14. Try to help your children achieve success in some way each day by offering a variety of activities.

15. Listen to your children and look them in the eyes when they are talking to you.

16. Do not set your expectations so high that the chance of failure prevents your children from trying.

17. Encourage your children to be proud of their name, ideas, and work. Pride makes a person try harder and strive to do better.

18. Give your children recognition for the effort they make even though it may not come up to your expectations. If you do this, the child will continue to try.

19. Answer your child's questions openly, honestly, and immediately, if possible.

20. Build a file of mementos of things in which your child has participated.

21. Point out the unique qualities in your children (skills, attitudes, behaviors, abilities, etc.) that make them special to you and others.

22. Do not compare one child to another.

23. Let your children know it's okay to express their feelings.

24. Let your children know that you love them even when you disapprove of their behavior. "I love you, but I don't like what you did." Discipline constructively, using positive suggestions, rather than destructively, using criticism.

lings); make no derogatory comments about the school, administration, principal, or faculty members; avoid confrontations; and remain neutral and objective.

Here are some additional ideas to consider in planning your conferences:

- Copy an article for parents or guardians that gives them suggestions on how to work with their child more effectively.

- Prepare a parent/guardian survey. Teachers might give parents or guardians a list of questions to think about prior to the conference or they could complete the survey and bring it with them. For example,

  o "Does your child like school? Why or Why not?"

  o "What are your child's interests?"

  o "Is there anything that you want me to know about your child?"

  o "What skills would you like your child to learn?"

  o "Are you satisfied with your child's progress?"

Henderson et al. (2007, p. 308) suggest some of the following questions:

  o Who is your child's best friend?

  o What are your child's successes in school?

  o What are your child's challenges?

  o What are some of your child's favorite activities?

  o How shall we stay in touch?

  o What are you hopes and dreams for your child this year?

- Establishing a positive dialogue with parents or guardians is important. However, if this seems to be a good time to discuss some areas of concern, the teacher must be mindful of the "positive theory of feedback." When discussing the student, the teacher should provide good news first, then areas of needed improvement, and then return to more good news. For example,

Teacher:	"Johnny really loves math. I'm sure that is his favorite subject."
Parent/Guardian:	"Yes, he's good in math."
Teacher:	"At times, he needs to be reminded to do his math homework. Do you have any ideas or suggestions that may help Johnny with his homework?"
Parent/Guardian:	"I can check to see that his homework is finished."
Teacher:	"Johnny is given time to write his homework assignment in his notebook. I can check to see that he writes it in the notebook. Could you sign the notebook when he has completed his homework?"
Parent/Guardian:	"Yes, I can go over his homework with him and sign his notebook each night."
Teacher:	"Thank you for your support. We want Johnny to be successful. I know we will have a great year."

- Use a simple student interest survey as a conversation starter at parent-or-guardian-teacher conferences. See Figures 4.6 and 4.7 for some sample student interest surveys. Place the survey on top of the student's work you will be discussing, and share some comments from the interest survey. It is a good icebreaker and demonstrates to the parents or guardians that you are interested in their child.

Student-Led Parent or Guardian Conferences

A student-led parent or guardian conference is another opportunity to involve parents in their children's education. This is an emerging trend in the middle schools. Choose a format that is comfortable for students, parents or guardians, and you. Students can begin by setting up a binder that contains graded work. The parents or guardians are notified that their child will lead the conference. Approximately a week before the conference, the student and teacher may want to update the binder and organize it to represent current assignments, tests, homework, and progress graphs. Some teachers have suggested students include in the binder a checklist of what to cover; a favorite assignment to discuss with parents or guardians; a few reflection paragraphs on their study skills, grades, and progress; and a list of ways to improve or challenge themselves in the next grading period or semester. At the following website, you can download a handbook on planning and implementing student-led conferences (**http://mlei.pbworks.com/f/SLCPP.pdf**).

VI. More Parent or Guardian Involvement Suggestions

A teacher must develop and implement ways to promote parent or guardian involvement. Many teachers suggest creating a parental interest form where parents or guardians can indicate areas of interest is a good place to start. The form could also list ways parents or guardians would like to get involved in their child's classroom. Some school system websites post preapproved sample letters such as an introductory letter and a letter requesting a conference. The website may also offer advice on conducting parent or guardian involvement events. Other suggestions from veteran teachers are outlined below. Read the suggestions carefully and choose the ones that interest you. Highlight the ideas you are planning to use. The suggestions are divided into three subtopics: Getting Parents or Guardians Involved, Using Parents or Guardians as Resources, and Involving Parents or Guardians as Homework Helpers. Without determination and careful planning, these ideas will stay on these pages and never get into your classroom.

Getting Parents or Guardians Involved

- Send parents or guardians a questionnaire asking how they would like to be involved, what concerns they have about their child's education, and what special skills they might be willing to contribute to the learning process or to the classroom. Henderson et al. (2007) include a sample high school parent volunteer survey in their book, ***Beyond the Bake Sale*** (pp. 308–311).

FIGURE 4.6   *Sample Student Interest Survey*

Interest Survey

What would you do if . . .

. . . you were President of the United States?

. . . you knew that you were going to be snowed in for a week?

. . . you could invite one friend to go with you to Disney World? Who would you invite? Why?

. . . you could trade lives with one person? Who would it be? Why?

. . . you were given one million dollars?

. . . you could have any job in the world?

. . . you could change one thing about yourself?

FIGURE 4.7   *Sample Student Interest Survey*

1. What subject do you enjoy the most? Why?

2. I like the way I acted when . . .

3. I would like to work on . . .

4. I feel good about . . .

5. I enjoy school because . . .

- Call parents or guardians on a regular basis to keep them informed of their child's progress and to keep the communication lines open. Schedule some time to make a certain number of phone calls each Monday evening.

- Ask parents or guardians for information on their child's learning style and for their observations about how the child learns best.

- Send home weekly progress reports. Design them to be interesting and something the parents or guardians look forward to receiving.

- Plan monthly or seasonal special events when students invite their parents or guardians to share in activities that represent the culmination of a unit of study.

- Schedule days when parents or guardians can come to school and walk through a day of school with their child. Plan this in conjunction with "Student of the Week" or "V.I.P." students.

- Hold monthly parent or guardian lunch days where parents or guardians eat lunch with their children in the classroom. Before the parents or guardians arrive, have the students decorate the tables with special tablecloths they made from art paper. Play soft music and make this a special event.

- Find creative ways to involve parents or guardians in planning class parties—activities that are not too demanding of time and finances but will make use of their own creativity. Support their ideas as much as possible.

- Schedule more parent-or-guardian-teacher conferences than are required, or plan "office hours" when you are available at regular times for parents or guardians to call you or walk in.

- Offer a door prize, drawing, or some incentive for coming to an open house or other event in your classroom. Be sure to publicize it among all the families.

- Explain to parents or guardians certain techniques for teaching, for making learning materials, or for planning lessons. Invite parents or guardians to an actual workshop taught by you.

- Hold a miniworkshop to teach parents or guardians and their children about book binding. Use cereal box front and back panels and cover with contact paper. Encourage parents or guardians to help their children make books about family jokes, family trips, and other family events.

- Have a parent or guardian with an interest and talent for developing center activities help you plan and create new activities each month.

- Plan and design a monthly newsletter format that includes an introduction of each month's instructional plans and themes, as well as items that parents or guardians may be able to donate. Include specific classroom events or duties for which parents or guardians can volunteer. Add parenting tips or items of interest and suggested reading for them and their children.

- Hold a video party for parents or guardians and students some evening after school. Show a video of a class activity and then a movie to enjoy. Provide popcorn and drinks.

- Hold a Saturday Family Activity where parents or guardians would relate something positive about their family life. Display family albums, family projects, family trees, family recipes (and samples). Invite some of your friends to attend and take family photos.

- Invite parents or guardians to share their hobbies with the class (e.g., crafts, coin collections, photography, stamp collections, sea shell collections, whittling, ham radio, sewing, or knitting).

Using Parents or Guardians as Resources

- Invite parents or guardians to the classroom to discuss their jobs, professions, or life experiences.

- Have parents or guardians bring in visual aids, such as a grocery list, store advertisements, and purchased groceries, when you discuss money, math, or consumer practices, and favorite ethnic folktales or foods when you study other cultures.

- Hold a multicultural fair and invite parents or guardians to come and be guest speakers. They might bring in ethnic food or arts and crafts. You may choose to have students and parents or guardians serve as the guest speakers, cooks, and crafters.

- Ask a volunteer to type stories or poetry the class has written and make eye-catching displays.

- Send activities home to a willing parent or guardians volunteer to cut, color, and paste for your centers or bulletin boards.

- Ask parents or guardians to take photos or videos of class work and projects to be shown at the end of the year or at a movie party.

- Involve parents or guardians in small-group instruction. You may provide training sessions so that they will present correct information and instruction and teach according to your philosophy.

- Invite a parent or guardian to assist one group of students with work after you have worked with them (e.g., the parent or guardian takes a reading group and helps to review and reinforce the skills while you work with another reading group).

- Have parents or guardians in the classroom as you teach a new skill or concept. During guided practice and independent practice, have parents and guardians monitor the work being done so that students are not completing assignments incorrectly.

- Invite parents or guardians to help with special projects. It's always nice to have extra hands for cutting, organizing, and distributing materials or answering questions.

- Invite parent or guardian volunteers into the classroom when you are working on creative writing. You assign the topic and ask students to make their own rough drafts. Then assign a parent or guardian volunteer to a group of five students. Have the students read their stories aloud and invite the parents and guardians to help in editing.

Involving Parents or Guardians as Homework Helpers

- Give an assignment asking parents or guardians to help their children write and draw pictures that would make up a short story. Plan a simple and non-threatening competition with awards for best story, original plot, imaginative art, or humor. Or you could hold the contest for stories written and illustrated by the parents or guardians, letting the children select the winners.

- Give a regular weekly assignment that requires the parent or guardian to work with the child. If some parents or guardians are not responsive, find a school resource teacher who would be a "substitute parent or guardian" for such assignments so that the children feel special.

- Give class assignments that require students to ask questions of their parents or guardians.

- Ask parents or guardians to write an original poem, story, or brief report and bring it to share with the class. Have the parents or guardians show the students the various steps they took in writing the piece so that students can see that even adults have to go through a process to write and revise. Then display the finished product the parent or guardian has shared.

- Ask parents or guardians to watch a particular television show with their children and discuss the show afterward.

- Ask parents or guardians to research upcoming television programming that may be of interest to the students or follow your instructional topics and themes. Ask a parent or guardian to record television programs for your class.

- Invite a parent or guardian to be your newsletter editor. Encourage him or her to call on other parents for input.

The teacher can communicate with parents and guardians and students through a class webpage, class newsletter, e-mails, and blogs. Many teachers are developing class webpages. You can share items such as school policies, schedules, special events, due dates, and other critical information pertaining to your class. Nelson and Bailey (2008, pp. 176–178) highlight information about designing class websites and what to include in a newsletter that are extremely helpful to teachers. Thompson (2008, p. 201) states that "the use of computer-mediated communication such as email over the last decade has reportedly increased the level of parental involvement at the elementary and secondary level." However, parent-or-guardian-teacher e-mail communication as well as teacher-student e-mailing raise important questions and concerns. Educators are urged to better understand the complexity associated with e-mail exchanges before getting involved.

Remember, the more parents and guardians you can get involved in your classroom, the more their children are likely to succeed in your classroom and in school. When students realize that their parents or guardians and teachers are working together, they are more likely to commit the time and energy needed for achieving academic goals.

CHAPTER FIVE

How Do I Begin the Year?

I. Teacher as a Manager

The school year has officially started and the children are coming down the hall to your class. I know you are wondering if you are ready for them and if you are ready for the school year to begin. During the first days and weeks of school, you need to concentrate on creating a positive learning environment. Many books and journal articles describe the experiences of first-year teachers; some focus on their fears and lack of experience, and others on how they need to look like they are in control (Bullough, 1989; Bullough & Baughman, 1997; Davis, Resta, Knox, & Anderson, 1998; Davis, Resta, Miller, & Fortman, 1999; Drayer, 1979; Grady, 1998; Hoak, 1999; Lovette, 1996; Ryan, 1970, 1986). However, few sources have specifically addressed how first-year teachers can plan their leap from the campus to the classroom.

The first day and weeks are critical times in the life of a new teacher. This is the time for you to establish your role in the classroom and to get to know your students. Smith (1993, p. 121) says, "It has become apparent during visits with former undergraduate students who were beginning a teaching career that success during the first month in the classroom was critical to future growth." Many researchers agree that all teachers, whether elementary, middle, or teaching at the secondary level, who spend considerable time during the first several weeks of school on classroom management, are considered more effective teachers (Emmer & Evertson, 2012; Evertson & Anderson, 1979; Evertson & Emmer, 2012; Hoak, 1999; Hubbard & Power, 1998; Lovette, 1996; McDaniel, 1986). Classroom management for all teachers begins with teaching rules, defining procedures, establishing consequences, developing incentives, and employing strategies and practices to support this effort. Good and Brophy (2007, p. 77) remind teachers that "effective management begins with planning the kind of learning environment that will support your intended curriculum."

In addition to developing and teaching rules, routines, cues, and procedures, first-year teachers must pay attention to other areas as well: creating a positive first impression, establishing a positive climate for learning, developing positive relationships with students, strengthening peer relationships, and forming effective ways to work with parents and guardians. (In thinking about parents and guardians, review Chapter 4 when the open house and parent-or-guardian-teacher conferences are scheduled.) Anderson (2004, p. 50) states that "to facilitate the task of classroom teaching, teachers need to create a psychological environment that is perceived positively and similarly by students." Good and Brophy (2007, p. 74) suggest teachers "get to know your students and show that you value them." A focus on "getting-acquainted" activities is important, and many such activities should be collected and used throughout the school year. Schell and Burden (2000) highlight many activities for teachers to use to begin the school year.

Let's take a look at some of the realities of the first day, weeks, and month of teaching. The first week is filled with lesson plans, interruptions, paperwork, and changes. The beginning teacher must create lesson plans for teaching and for the management plan as well. (See Figure 5.1, based on the authors' lesson plan paradigm of Hunter, 1989.) Save the lesson plans on your computer in folders with appropriate topic designations as you may have to reteach and revise them.

FIGURE 5.1   *Sample of a Lesson Plan Format*

Planned Lessons and Activities

- **Topic**–Recognize Adjectives

- **Opener**–Hook the learner. The ***opener*** must create interest, stimulate enthusiasm, and engage the learner.

   Provide a description of a pet, incident, or the school principal without adjectives and then with adjectives. Ask students which they liked better and why.

- **Objectives**–The student will be able to

   1. Define adjectives

   2. Identify adjectives in sentences

   3. Create a paragraph using at least six adjectives

   In writing objectives, use action verbs that are measurable from six cognitive domains from Bloom's (1984) Taxonomy.

   Begin by focusing the students' attention to the objectives of the lesson written on the board. You are saying, "This is what the teacher is going to teach and this is what the student is going to learn."

   - **Instruction**–Ten to fifteen minutes of a mini-lecture using teaching strategies for ***each*** objective.

   - **Guided practice**–Students practice the information independently or in pairs or groups after each objective's instruction. This is an ***ungraded*** activity.

- **Assessment**–The teacher assesses the students' understanding after each objective by monitoring the guided practice activity. The teacher makes the decision to move to the next objective or stay with the current objective and provide more instruction, examples, or practice activities based on students' learning of the material.

  Instruction, guided practice activity, and assessment must be provided with each objective. Do not teach all the objectives at once. Provide guided practice for each objective individually.

  The chart below provided an example of differentiated instruction at the elementary and middle school level, and working with special populations.

Whole-Group Instruction *Students below grade level* 1. Five problems	**Whole-Group Instruction** *Students at grade level* 2. Ten Problems	**Whole-Group Instruction** *Students above grade level* 3. Integrate another subject into the assignment.
Example . . . *Subject–Science:* Label the food pyramid and find, cut, and paste one picture next to each level.	**Example . . .** *Subject–Science:* Draw and label the food pyramid and find, cut, and paste three examples for each level. Answer the prepared handout of ten questions.	**Example . . .** *Subject–Science:* Draw and label the food pyramid. Make a brochure discussing the food pyramid for good health and keep a journal of what you eat and from what groups for a week.
Activity *Learning Centers–Table I* Rotate centers every ten minutes or so. Group A–Teacher provides reading material and discusses a topic with student group. Groups rotate tables.	**Activity** *Learning Centers–Table II* Group B–Draw and label the parts of a plant. Write two sentences about the importance of plants.	**Activity** *Learning Centers–Table III* Group C–Place a plant in the soil pot and place your name on the pot. Put on the windowsill with a stick label with a date planted.
Whole-Group Instruction Inclusion–Special Populations: Use IEP information to adjust assignment given.	**Whole-Group Instruction** Regular Education Students: Assignment given–no modifications.	**Whole-Group Instruction** Gifted Education: Same or different assignment given with multiple tasks and choices.

- **Closure**–*Refocus* students' attention on the objectives. The purpose of the closure is to help the students conceptualize what they have learned in class. Have students tell you what they have learned. It is a reflection for the students on their lesson, block, day.

- **Independent Practice**–Students complete an assignment independently on in pairs or groups and the work can be *graded*.

Another reality is the enormous amount of paperwork that needs to be completed during the first few days of school. Many first-year teachers report that the paperwork was overwhelming and the priority it took was astounding. One first-year teacher made this following comment that offers beginning teachers some needed encouragement: "Even though the first few days in the classroom are difficult, try and look on the bright side, as it can only get better."

Management must begin the year; management must be maintained throughout the year; and management must end the year. Be assured that having a plan for managing the class will definitely help you with the realities of the first days. Teaching the class rules, procedures, routines, consequences, and incentives are major management tasks for beginning teachers. You must develop management lesson plans that will teach your students how the class will work from day to day. You must teach and model the techniques that encourage appropriate student and class behavior. Using positive reinforcement such as the *positive ripple effect* and *catch-them-being-good technique* are two important management strategies to encourage and maintain appropriate and expected student behavior. Here are examples of using these strategies: "Mary, I like the way you have your journal on your desk and are ready to start this activity," and "Jack, thank you for coming into the room quietly from your bathroom break."

The following classroom management plan was developed to help first-year teachers get off to a good start by becoming effective classroom managers. This comprehensive plan incorporates tried and true ideas and strategies experienced teachers have found to be successful with learners of all abilities, all grade levels, and cultures. The following codes will help you identify suggestions that work well with special student populations. Look for the appropriate code in the management plan to quickly access information specific to your situations and meet your specific classroom needs and student challenges.

- ✤ **special education (inclusion and self-contained)**
- ✦ **middle school specific**
- ★ **secondary specific**
- ✱ **culturally diverse learners**

The first-year general education teacher in the elementary, middle, and secondary settings can implement the 30-day plan as written. Some modifications may be necessary, however, for the coded populations listed above.

✤ *Special Education (Inclusion and Self-Contained) Specific*

The first-year special education teacher may want to read this information before beginning the 30-day plan. Each student will have an individualized education plan

(IEP) with goals, objectives, and accommodations to help the special education student access the curriculum. When working with special student populations, it is most important for teachers to realize that organizational deficits are common characteristics for students with learning disorders, behavioral disorders, and ADHD (Smith, Polloway, & Dowdy, 2007). This means that students may have difficulty maintaining an assignment (planner) book, keeping track of their books and book bags, and placing their papers in order. Salend (2010) suggests using many visuals, such as charts, webs, or time lines, and presenting things orally to the students. In response to multiple learning styles, Kottler, Kottler and Kottler (2004, pp. 71–72) suggest "breaking assignments into smaller chunks, using graphic organizers, narrowing the focus to key terms and concepts, allowing extra time for completion of tasks, using the computer or other assistive technologies, and having someone else write for them."

Many special education teachers working in inclusion classrooms suggest the need for the general education and the special education teachers to spend time at the beginning of the year getting to know each other to develop a strong working relationship. It is helpful to assign class tasks to one another, such as taking attendance and developing warm-up activities. Lesson plans can be developed together and responsibility for certain components of the lesson assigned. It is hoped that in an inclusion classroom, an observer would not know who is the general education teacher and who is the special education teacher.

In working together, the special education and the general education teachers receive goal pages and accommodations for each special education student in the class from the student's case manager. It's the special education teacher's job to make sure that the special education students receive their accommodations (for example, the use of a calculator). The general education teacher may be asked to attend the student's IEP meetings. The special education teacher should help the general education teacher with ideas for meeting the needs, accommodations, and goals of special education students in inclusion settings. The student's IEP manager may consult with the both the special education and the general education teachers on how the student is reaching and progressing toward the identified goals and suggest ways to push the student toward their postsecondary or career goals.

In addition, special education teachers must take the time to get to know their assigned paraeducators/teacher assistant. In self-contained special education classrooms, the paraeducators/teacher assistant needs the same IEP information as the special education teacher. They also need suggestions for working with the special education students. Take the time to share expectations and discuss each person's role. Special education teachers suggest meeting with their paraeducators/teacher assistant each week to discuss their successes and challenges and interactions with students. Regular communications, along with keeping a pulse on expectations, are of great value in accomplishing student goals.

✦ ★ *Middle and Secondary School Specific*

The middle and secondary students will not have a full day's schedule as outlined below. Your outline would conclude after the morning. You may get a new group of students in the afternoon and repeat the morning outline or you may have many different students in a block or bell situation. However, read the rest of the day's activities to see what you may want to include that same day or use the next day. Zuckerman (2007) presents proactive classroom discipline strategies for secondary teachers to consider. Most of the strategies are the same for all teachers at any level. Many of the preventive and proactive management strategies are covered in the following 30-day management plan, for example, lesson plans, classroom rules, routines, and cues. Feel free to adapt, combine, delete, and add to this first-month management plan. The plan is rather detailed, but it gradually decreases in intensity, allowing the academics to take priority.

✱ *Culturally Diverse Learner Specific*

For teachers working with diverse student populations, a popular classroom management strategy, such as "Look at me" or asking for eye contact, may not be appropriate. Johns and Espinoza's (1996) ***Management Strategies for Culturally Diverse Classroom*** offers many suggestions and examples for working more appropriately and specifically with diverse populations.

Bosch (2006) explains that by developing and implementing a classroom management plan, the teacher is providing structure to everything that goes on in the classroom—from the first day to the last. Your classroom management plan needs to be supported by students who know each other, are able to work together, and are willing to learn together. The classroom management plan must be taught, not just told, to the students. The students must know and feel its importance. They must see that this plan is a democratic classroom approach for the teacher and students to work and learn together. Remember the teacher must review, reinforce, and reteach the management plan as needed in order to ensure success throughout the year. Veteran teachers should remind beginning teachers to review the management plan, especially after the holidays and any school breaks.

II. The 30-Day Classroom Management Plan

First Week

First Week Goal: Teach What Is Important

Key Teaching Areas

- ☐ Teach management plan.
- ☐ Establish and teach routines.

❏ Establish and teach cues.

❏ Model procedures.

❏ Develop and teach rules.

❏ Develop and teach correction plan.

❏ Develop positive teacher-student relationships.

❏ Develop student accountability.

Strategies for Success

❏ Provide get-acquainted activities.

❏ Use positive ripple effect.

❏ Offer praise, feedback, and encouragement.

Self-Reflective Opportunities

❏ Maintain a daily or weekly journal on the computer and add reflections at the end of the day or week, prior to leaving school. The entries should showcase teaching highlights and stumbling blocks. Make a list of those students needing encouragement. Remember to include all student populations (♣ ◆ ★ ✳). Review code descriptions on preceding page.

Reminders for First Day

✓ Introductory letter

✓ Index cards

✓ Orientation folders

✓ Student's supply list

✓ Name tags or puzzle pieces

✓ Cue signals—whistle, bell

Most schools have a four-day work week to begin the school year. This management plan begins with a four-day approach. If you begin with a five-day work week, spread the activities for the four days outlined over the five days.

Day 1—First Impression

BEGIN THE DAY: Greet the students at the door, introduce yourself, and ask their names, shake their hands, and tell them how happy you are to have them in your class. **(✳) Greeting second language learners at the door with a word or phrase in their native language is special.** The class will say or hear the Pledge of Allegiance and have a silent moment. Many times this is done as a schoolwide activity over the loud speaker or closed circuit television.

OPENING ACTIVITIES: Direct the students to the bulletin board to obtain their name tags. The students will be wearing their name tags or displaying them on their desks during the first day or days. At the end of each day, they will return the name tags to the bulletin board. The bulletin board could be a tree stating, "You are the apple of my eye," with name tags shaped like apples, or "Mrs. Jones's Class Tree," with name tags shaped like leaves. If assigned seating is part of your plan, have students match the number placed on the name tags to the number on the seat. This provides a fun activity for sharing names and gives you a seating chart from which to begin your first day.

(♦) An opening activity *for middle school students* could be to create a name tent for their desk or design name plates similar to personalized license plates. The students are given scrap paper to write down ideas. The name plates may have no more than eight letters. The student chooses one plate idea and is then given colored paper and a magic marker to make the plate. The plate is placed on tag board that is folded at the bottom so it can be taped to the front of the desk. The students share why they chose their plates. The teacher makes a name plate, too. The name plates can be placed on a bulletin board titled "Licensed to Learn!"

OR

In another activity, the teacher makes a large puzzle and places one student's name on each puzzle piece. (The teacher can make several copies of each puzzle piece to use for other activities.) The student is directed to come into the room and go to the back table to find a puzzle piece with his or her name on it. The student is to find the seat—the one that has the same puzzle piece taped to it. When everyone has come into the room, the teacher will give the students approximately ten to fifteen minutes to put the puzzle together on the back table. The teacher will preserve the puzzle, post it in the room for all to see, and then refer to it to encourage students—especially "loners"—to work together. Discuss with the students the idea that things work better together than apart ("two heads are better than one"). The third set of puzzle pieces can be used to call on students randomly when too many hands are raised. The pieces can be put in a can and drawn out by the teacher or a student.

(★) An opening activity for secondary students could be to interview each other. They could develop a list of at least ten questions and draw a person's name out of a hat to interview and introduce to the class.

INTRODUCTION: Introduce yourself to the class. Then write the word *fun* on the board. Begin the activity by saying, "I'm going to give you a minute to think about this question, 'What is fun?' and then I am going to ask for your thoughts." Watch the clock and when the time is up, make eye contact with students and ask for responses. Next say, "I'm going to give you another minute to think about this question, 'Why is it fun?'" After some discussion, have the students summarize the "what and why of fun" and begin sharing your teaching philosophy, which includes fun. Discuss your expectations for a positive year.

(★) A secondary education idea might be to introduce yourself in a unique way that reveals your goals and expectations for the course and class. Ask the students to write down their goals and expectations for the course and class and have a class discussion. You may want to continue brainstorming and develop ways to get teacher and student goals in alignment.

GUIDELINES: Discuss the following: lunch money, bus numbers, use of bathroom passes, when to sharpen pencils, and when to throw away trash. Require a standard behavior to line up, to walk in the halls, and to eat in the lunchroom. **(◆) For middle school students, discuss some of the following: how to enter the classroom, the daily warm-up procedures, how to turn in homework, and where to place notes from parents or guardians.** Use a procedure for the required behavior and use the positive ripple effect to support the procedure. For example, say "I like the way row 1 is ready for the lineup. They may go first," "I like the way Jimmy walked to his place in line," and "Kate, you were so quick to get in line. Thanks!"

(◆★) Middle and secondary students prefer the positive ripple effect to be used for group acknowledgment such as by groups, rows, or gender, rather than individuals chosen by the teacher.

Use many different selection methods for lining up and for grouping students. One method is to assign a day of the week to each row and on that day that row lines up first. Other methods include lining up by type of shoes, birthday months, clothing, favorite TV shows, foods, eye color, number of pets, number of brothers and sisters, last year's teachers, and so on.

OPENING TASKS: Let students know what the materials are needed for class, such as notebooks, pencils, assignment book, student planner, crayons, or scissors. Distribute a list of needed supplies at the end of the day. For younger students, place names and bus numbers on large, cutout bus posters and put them in the room near the door.

ESTABLISH A CUE: Teach a cue to gain the students' attention. Use this cue from this day forward. Wait for their attention and begin when you have everyone's attention. Tell the students the cues will be used at various times to get everyone's attention quickly and especially when the teacher is ready to begin instruction. Again, support this procedure by looking for the positive. Find the students or row or table-top individuals who are doing the "right" things and praise, reward, and reinforce the behavior you want to continue. Five interesting and effective cues are as follows:

1. A bell, wind chimes, whistle, clap, lights on and off. (♣ ✳)

2. A stoplight: the red light means stop, look, and listen; yellow—too noisy, quiet down; and green—great job. (♣ ✳)

3. A signal, an object (hat, lab coat), sign language, one-word cue. One first-year teacher asked her students to choose a word or group of words as a cue to begin class, such as "Freeze, Look, and Listen." The students had ownership of the cue and responded quickly. (♣ ✳)

4. A rap that the class composes or a clap sequence to begin class. Teacher starts and all join in as they prepare for class and to focus on the teacher. (♦)

5. Raise a hand and move to the front of the room. (♣ ★ ✳)

Planned Lessons and Activities (♦ ★)

Use the established cue to gain everyone's attention. Teach the first lesson in your management plan. The subject of the lesson is how the students will start the school day. This includes the first classroom rule and the routine procedure to begin the school day.

- **Topic**–Rule 1: Be Ready for Class
  Discuss and teach your first rule and expectation for the class.

- **Opener**–Plan a short role-play. Tell the students that you will be going out of the room and entering again and you want them to tell you all the things they see that are wrong. Come into the class very unprepared. Be rushing, without materials, upset, can't find your lesson plan book, left the quote for the day at home, the graded papers to be returned to students as promised cannot be found, and hurriedly give the students some work to keep them busy without any instructions or teaching of material.

- **Objectives**–The student will be able to
  1. Identify how to be ready for class
  2. Resolve situations in which they are unprepared for class

- **Instruction**–Web the word *unprepared*. The students identify all the examples of the teacher being unprepared for class. Discuss with students how they have expectations for you and you have expectations for them. Web around the words, *Be Ready for Class*. The students discuss how they can be ready for class. Discuss teacher expectations for entering the room. Discuss readiness tasks, such as turning in papers, lunch-money procedure, taking attendance, turning in notes from parents or guardians, putting away lunch boxes, hanging up coats, and preparing for class (e.g., sharpening pencils and getting notebooks). Middle school students need a locker procedure and practice on how to open their locks. In addition, discuss when to sharpen pencils during the school day or where to get pencils and paper if needed.

- **Guided Practice**–Students copy the word webs, which are to be collected and placed in the orientation folders that will be made later in the day.

- **Assessment**–Present scenarios for when a rule is broken—for example, forgetting books, pencil, or paper. Listen to assess student accountability.

- **Closure**–Why is it important to be ready for class?

The teacher continues to teach the management plan with a discussion of why rules are important to the class. The teacher must reinforce the concept that RULES ALLOW and DO NOT RESTRICT (see Figure 5.2).

(✣) **A suggestion from a special education teacher reveals the importance for this special population to have rules that can be generalized and apply to more than the classroom. She shares this:**

> **It is important that the rules don't apply just to the four walls (classroom) around them, but are rules they are expected to follow everywhere. I have one rule—No rules, just do right. I spend considerable time teaching what "right" means in all school situations. For example, the class discusses what "right" means in being on time (ready for class to start) or being patient (waiting for people to finish talking before you begin to talk).**

Planned Lessons and Activities (✦ ★)

- **Topic**–Our Classroom Rules

- **Opener**–Review the first rule of the class: Be ready for class. Suggest the class discuss why rules are to allow and not restrict or why rules are important. Provide examples such as "right on red," or playing sports without a referee.

- **Objectives**–The student will be able to
  1. List three reasons why rules are important
  2. Develop four more rules that will help me teach and you learn

FIGURE 5.2   *Classroom Rules*

Develop classroom rules:

1. Use approximately five rules.
2. State them clearly.
3. Make them short and easy to memorize.
4. State them positively.
5. Get a commitment to the rules (show of hands, vote, contract, bulletin board display).
6. Teach each rule (share expectations).

Teach classroom rules:

1. Involve the students in the development of the rules.
2. Discuss and internalize their value.
3. Discuss expectations.
4. Get student agreement and commitment to rules (vote, contract).
5. Teach rules.
6. Model rules.
7. Review rules.
8. Reinforce rules.
9. Monitor whether, or which, rules have been learned.
10. Reteach if necessary.
11. Enforce rules.
12. Discuss consequences for not following the rules.

Sample rules:

1. Be prepared. 2. Be cooperative. 3. Be respectful. 4. Be responsible.	1. Be prepared to learn. 2. Encourage others. 3. Use quiet voices. 4. Give full attention to the teacher when he or she is speaking.
1. Be prepared for class. 2. Treat each other fairly. 3. Follow teacher requests. 4. Obey all school rules. 5. Work to do your best.	1. Come to class prepared to work and learn. 2. Be considerate of others. 3. Respect others' property. 4. Speak with an inside voice. 5. Obey all school rules.

Set up procedures for the following:

- Routines for the beginning of the school day, ending of the school day

- Cues for gaining student attention

- Turning in assignments (in proper basket)

- Handing notes to the teacher (in the special basket on the teacher's desk)

- Turning in late work

- Using notebooks for each subject (taking notes)

- Appropriate times to sharpen pencils

- Using passes—hall, bathroom, office, nurse

- Appropriate auditorium and lunchroom behavior

- Fire drills

- Classroom visitors

- Doing make-up work due to illness

- Solving problems

- Giving directions (see instructions in the management plan)

- **Instruction**–Ask students what they think would happen if two teams were playing baseball and there were no rules, coach, or umpire. List answers on the board. Discuss rules and why they are important. For older students, discuss car driving rules such as right on red. Continue by telling them that you selected the first rule, Be ready for class, and that they are going to choose the four additional rules for this class. Discuss the need for rules to be clearly and positively stated, short in length, and easy to memorize.

    For younger students, you can discuss ways to make a happy class. On the chalkboard, list three to five ways they can have a happy, safe class.

- **Guided Practice**–For older students, assign students to groups of four and ask each group to think of four rules that are needed in this classroom. Give a time limit for the work to be completed. Instead of group work, each student can write four more rules he or she would like to have in the classroom. Discuss and list these rules on the chalkboard. Then let the students select the rules and agree on them. Take a vote for commitment to the class rules. Students or teacher will make a poster or bulletin of the class rules.

- **Assessment**–Listen to discussion and observe poster

- **Closure**–Why are rules important? Give me three reasons. How can rules help me teach? How can rules help you learn?

- **Independent Practice**–Write the five rules to include in orientation folders.

ESTABLISH AFTER-LUNCH IDEA: Read-aloud time. Select reading material to read to the class for approximately fifteen minutes. Decide what you want the students to do while you read. Many students like to have a copy of the book you are reading so they can follow along.

(♣ ✳) If you have attention-span issues with your special student populations, you may want to read in three-minute intervals allowing for questions. Have someone rotating as a pointer if you read a big book or have them act out what they just heard. Higher-functioning students may only need a book to follow along with the reading.

ACTIVITY: Have each student begin to make an orientation folder of information pertaining to this class. The folder can contain handouts, notes, a schedule of the day, a calendar, school policies and rules, important dates, and curriculum highlights. The student adds information and assignments to the folder throughout the week. The folders are kept in a special location in the room. At completion of the folder, the students sign a contract that they understand their personal role in the teaching and learning process and also understand the operation of the class and the teacher's management plan that will maximize student learning and minimize disruptive student behavior. **For special student populations, you may want to include how this information applies to the real world, such as in a work environment.**

The students take home the orientation folders during the second week of school and familiarize their parents or guardians with the class process. Parents or guardians sign a statement that the student has briefed them concerning the classroom management plan.

ACTIVITY: Distribute the *More About Me* activity (Figure 5.3) for the orientation folder to the students. The teacher may want to complete this questionnaire as well. Your responses may match some of your students' responses and this, then, becomes an even stronger relationship-building exercise. Circulate around the room as they complete this assignment. Ask them to share their feelings. For younger elementary students, this can be done orally, or they can draw pictures. Older elementary students can write a descriptive paragraph about how they feel about school and learning. Collect the assignment and read responses; later put the questionnaire, picture, or paragraph in the orientation folder.

FIGURE 5.3   *Activity for the Orientation Folder*

More About Me

1. What is your favorite holiday and why do you like it?

2. Who is your favorite friend? Why?

3. What is your favorite color?

4. What is your favorite thing to eat?

5. What is your favorite thing to do?

6. Tell about a special gift you have received from someone.

7. What is something you have never done and would like to try? Why?

8. Tell about a good dream.

9. What is your favorite book and why do you like it?

10. What makes you mad?

The teacher may want to complete this form and share with the class.

Get-acquainted activities are important in promoting class cohesiveness. It is important to have get-acquainted activities throughout the school year. The **Get to Know Your Classmates** planned lesson below can be used in most classroom settings.

(✳) **To be a culturally responsible classroom teacher, use the common game** *Find Someone* . . . **(e.g., find someone from another country, find someone whose parents are from another country, or find someone who has a custom or tradition similar to yours) as a get-acquainted activity (Weinstein, Curran, & Tomlinson-Clark, 2003).**

(✦ ★) **For middle and secondary students, try these get-acquainted activities:** *Two Truths and a Lie* **or** *Little-Known Facts About Me*. **In Two Truths and a Lie, the students in the class write down two statements that are true about themselves and one statement that is a lie. The student reads them to the class and they decide which statement is the lie. A variation of this activity is Little-Known Facts About Me, in which a student writes a statement about themselves that they think others won't know and students draw these statements out of a box and guess who it is (Sapon-Shevin, 1999).**

Planned Lessons and Activities (♣ ✦ ★)

Use the established cue to gain everyone's attention.

- **Topic**–Get to Know Your Classmates

- **Opener**–How do you feel when you walk into a room and you don't know anyone? How do you feel when you go somewhere and you see lots of your friends?

- **Objectives**–The student will be able to

  1. Identify three reasons for getting to know other classmates
  2. Name and know something about two, four, or six classmates

- **Instruction**–Begin by asking the students if they know everyone in the class. Ask a specific student to name as many of the students as possible. Discuss why it is important to know each other in the class—they are more comfortable, accepted, more like a group, and so on.

- **Guided Practice**–Get-acquainted activities–See Figures 5.3, 5.4, 5.5, and 5.6 for examples of such activities. Teachers can help students make connections to one another through such interests as travel or pets (working for group cohesiveness, a sense of family).

FIGURE 5.4 *Ideas for Get-Acquainted Activities*

Eight Get-Acquainted Activities

1. Play class-names BINGO.

2. Show-and-Tell Suitcase: Student gives name, destination, and one item to take on the trip. Each student repeats what has been said before and adds his or her name and an item.

3. Name Chain: Students sit in a circle and share their names and something about themselves or a way others can remember them or their names. A ball of string or a bean bag can be used to toss to the next student to share. Suggest that students remember who they toss the string to for making a bulletin board display of this activity.

4. Interview classmates.

5. Scavenger Hunt: Find out things about classmates: Who has a cat? Who has a birthday in April?

6. Find a Friend: Write down three things about yourself and find classmates who have the same things in common with you.

7. Prepare forms that have items written on then to find out about classmates.

8. Collect signatures of students who agree with certain written statements, such as "I like baseball," "I try to do my very best," and "I always turn on the radio when I study." Students and teachers can create these statements.

FIGURE 5.5   *Get-Acquainted Activity*

Let's Get Acquainted

Try to use the names of all our classmates to fill in the boxes.

For example, look at the first box. It says: Has black hair. Find a student with black hair. Write the student's name in that box.

1. Has black hair	2. Middle name is the same as yours	3. Favorite color is blue
4. Loves to write	5. Likes vegetables	6. Shoe size in the same as yours
7. Has a cat	8. Is taller than you are	9. Is wearing tennis shoes
10. Plays a sport	11. Went to the zoo this summer	12. Wants to be famous
13. Has a garden	14. Likes to draw	15. Has an older brother

FIGURE 5.6 *Interview Me*

In pairs, take turns asking each other the following ten questions.

Write the responses on a piece of paper. Circle the similar responses. Chart your similarities and differences. Class data can be graphed and placed on a bulletin board. You may want students to make two of their own questions.

1. What are your favorite school subjects?

2. What is your favorite sport to play?

3. What makes you happy?

4. How many pets do you have?

5. What is your favorite movie? Why?

6. What kinds of food do you like to eat?

7. What is something you have never done before?

8. What countries have you visited?

9. What do you like most about your school? Why?

10. What do you like to do after school?

- **Assessment**–Question and Answer: Assess how many students' names and connections are recalled.

- **Closure**–Begin by asking, "John, why is it important to know people in this class? Mary, tell me the name of one of the friends we learned about today or the four friends we got to know today? Tell the class something about one or all four." Ask a few students to name these friends and tell something they learned about them. Tell them they will do this activity each day until everyone knows everyone else by name and knows something about each person.

  Each time you repeat this activity, review the names of the students previously spotlighted by having those students stand up at the beginning of the activity. Quiz the class to see if they can remember their names and something about them.

ACTIVITY: Set aside some time to take the students on a tour of the school. Help students become familiar with the different areas in the school: office, library, gym. In addition, show them the offices of the counselor, nurse, custodian, secretary, and principal. Help the younger students learn their names. The final stop can be the cafeteria as you take them to lunch.

(♣) **When working with special education students, a teacher may want to have the students complete a very basic map of the school and label certain rooms and add some names of school personnel. They can color it and the teacher can laminate it for the student's pocket.**

ESTABLISH A ROUTINE FOR THE END OF THE DAY: Closure is a must for each lesson taught as well as to the end of every day. Set aside ten to fifteen minutes each day: for younger students, possibly once just before lunch and again before the end of the day; for older elementary students, once at the end of the day; for middle school learners at the end of the block; and for the secondary students at the end of the block or bell.

Simple closure activities include the following: "Tell me one thing you learned today." "Tell me what you enjoyed most today." "Tell me something you learned today that you want to tell your mom, dad, brother, sister, or friend." "Tell me something you learned today that your brother or sister doesn't know." "Tell me something interesting about science." "Tell me something you are thinking about when I say . . . (pick a topic taught during the day)."

Then ask them to complete these thoughts about today's learning: "Today I learned . . . , I relearned . . . , and I wish . . . ."

(✦ ★) **A reflective closure activity especially relevant to middle and secondary students utilizes the following shapes: the triangle, square, and circle. The triangle is asking if the student now sees the material from a different angle or in a different** way. **The square is asking if the student is squared away with the material and could teach it to another person. The circle is asking if there are still some unanswered questions going around in the student's head. The teacher can use one shape at a time or two or three or by individual, pair, or group. You could share individually, share by shape, or group students by shape and share responses.**

GUIDELINES: Pass out an introductory letter (Figure 5.7) to go home to the parents and guardians and attach it to the prepared list of materials and supplies needed for class.

REMINDERS:

- ✓ Identify several classroom routines.

- ✓ Label trays or baskets to collect students' work. Use labels such as *Teacher, In, Homework,* as well as labels for subjects such as Math or English. The Teacher basket is for notes from parents and guardians, attendance sheets, and homework recording forms.

- ✓ Prepare a poster of rules.

FIGURE 5.7   *Introductory Letter*

Dear Parents or Guardians,

Welcome to the _____ grade! I look forward to an exciting year of teaching and a great year of learning. I am interested in making this a successful and happy year for you and your child. To ensure this success, we must keep the lines of communication open. If you have any questions or concerns, please feel free to contact me at school until 4:00 p.m. each day. If you leave a message and a phone number, I will return the call as soon as possible. (Or you can reach me by e-mail at _____.)

In a few weeks our school will have its annual Open House night. At that time, I will discuss the academic program and my goals and expectations for the year. I encourage you to attend this special evening so that you can become better acquainted with the _____ grade program.

Sincerely,

Teacher's Name

✓ Read the More About Me worksheet.

✓ Prepare a map of the school.

✓ Get a journal that someone has written to read to the class. (Make sure you have asked if you can read the entry or if the student will read the entry to the class.) Don't let the class know ahead of time who will be selected to read.

(♣ ✳) **By including special student populations, this activity could remove labels and boost self-esteem and peer acceptance in a classroom. Remember to ask students if they are interested in reading their entries. Work with students one-on-one for the reading aloud experience. This could also be recorded for the classroom to hear.**

Day 2—Set High Expectations

BEGIN THE DAY: Greet the students at the door. Say something positive to each one as students walk into the room.

OPENING ACTIVITIES: Place reminders on the board for the students to follow.

1. Get your name tags.

2. Get ready for class.

3. Sit in your seat.

4. Be ready to say or hear the Pledge of Allegiance and have a silent moment.

ESTABLISH A ROUTINE PROCEDURE AND ACTIVITY TO BEGIN EACH DAY: Establish what the students need to do each day when they come into the classroom. This procedure remains the same throughout the year. The morning routine procedure is for the students to get ready for class upon entering the room.

Many teachers start each day with tasks the students must do to be prepared to begin the school day. Then, they establish a routine activity, such as quotes to read, discuss, and evaluate; comics to be shared; journals to be kept; or a silent sustained reading activity. (Other routine activities and procedures are listed in Figure 5.8.)

You need to establish and teach at least three routine procedures and activities: one to begin the day, one after lunch, and one to end the day. The routine activity for beginning the day in this management plan is journal writing. For younger students, you may want them to do a picture web in which you introduce a word, and the students draw pictures of what the word means to them.

(♦) **For middle school students, procedures are crucial as they need structure. Most of the time, middle school students don't like to be told what to do but rather just like to know what to do.**

FIGURE 5.8   *Routine Activities and Procedures*

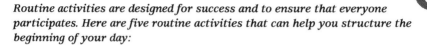

Routine activities are designed for success and to ensure that everyone participates. Here are five routine activities that can help you structure the beginning of your day:

1. Write in a journal.

2. Write the quote for the day and what the quote means to you.

3. Write the learning objective for the day in a notebook.

4. Write in a vocabulary notebook the vocabulary words for the day.

5. Use sustained silent reading time.

After-lunch routine procedures can include these eight:

1. Read-aloud time (story)

2. Sustained silent reading

3. Reports and discussion of current events

4. Social issue discussion

5. Free time or catch-up time

6. Student focus

7. Independent time (to use the computer, go to a learning center, go to the library, or read)

8. Committee work for class project

Five possible end-of-the-day routine procedures can include

1. Closure activity—"Tell me what you learned today or what the best thing you learned today."

2. Review of activities, trivia strategy, or games

3. Writing homework assignments in notebooks

4. Free time/catch-up time

5. Writing in a learning log

(✤ ✺) For special student populations, remember to have them draw a picture of what the procedure may look like, and write or tell a teacher what it means in their own words.

Begin the day by teaching the routine procedure and activity. Lead the students through the routine procedure of getting ready for class and writing (modeling) in their journals. The content of the lesson might be learning the value of journal writing.

You could begin to teach them about several people who have kept journals and how that has influenced history, science, and other people as well as their own lives. An activity might be making a cover for their journals and recording entry dates for the first month. The routine procedure is used to begin the day, begin the block of time, or begin the subject matter course.

USE CUE: Use a cue—such as a raised hand—and move to the front of the room. Get everyone's attention before beginning to teach the lesson or give out information. Use strong and direct eye contact for compliance.

(♣ ✳) You may want to tap a student or some students to let them know the cue is coming or whisper to them that you are ready to begin and to watch for the cue. This gives the student a sense of control. This helpful heads-up is important when working with students with special needs.

GUIDELINES: Teach the students the fire drill first: lights out, windows closed, door closed, the line-up procedure (by rows), and the route out of the building and to the designated area outside of building. Have a mock fire drill to practice procedures.

Many special education teachers tell me that this special population needs to be taught a fire drill procedure one-on-one as this is an uncomfortable and possibly upsetting topic for them. For the line-up procedure, tell students to remember who belongs in front and back of them so they can report if anyone is missing when they get to the designated area outside. Students can find their buddies once they reach that area. If the school requires other safety procedures, they should be introduced in the morning sometime during the first week of school.

Planned Lessons and Activities (♣ ✦ ★ ✳)

Use the established cue to gain everyone's attention. Teach one or two classroom rules a day until all rules have been taught. Rules should be taught just as if they were curriculum topics. Plan the lesson to include Topic, Opener, Objectives, Instruction, Discussion, Activities, Check for Understanding, Guided Practice, Closure, and Independent Practice. The next lesson to teach includes the second rule of showing respect for one another.

- **Topic**–Rule 2: Show Respect to One Another

- **Opener**–Brainstorm for ideas about the word *respect*. Explore such ideas as being polite, helping others, treating others fairly, not touching others' property, and the golden rule.

- **Objectives**–The student will be able to

  1. Define the word *respect*
  2. Demonstrate respect in various situations
  3. Provide examples of respect

- **Instruction**–The students read and discuss the definition of respect. The teacher puts two columns on the board: *What is respect?* and *What is disrespect?* The teacher presents situations such as showing respect or not showing respect at home, in school, on the playground, and so on. Together the teacher and students complete the chart on the board. Next, the teacher presents a situation and asks if this is a situation where respect is shown. Ask students to show a thumbs up, stand up, or raise their hands if respect is shown. Scan the class and if the majority understands, move to the next objective—provide examples.

- **Guided Practice**–Students create examples of respect or disrespect. The younger students can give examples of respect. Older students can work in pairs and write two or more examples of respect or disrespect on index cards. Then they can share or role-play a few examples. Collect the cards to use for reviewing the rule.

- **Assessment**–Listen to student-created examples and allow time for a question-and-answer period.

- **Closure**–How can you show respect to the teacher? How can you show respect to your classmates? How can respect be a part of our class?

- **Independent Practice**–Give older students an assignment to look for two examples of respect and disrespect (at home, in sports, etc.). Tell them the class will discuss their examples the next day.

ACTIVITY: Distribute textbooks, if available, the first or second day. Then introduce the students to the new textbooks. Along with the textbooks, give out an index card to each student. Have them write their name at the top of the cards and then list each book received and its inventory number. Collect the cards.

Have each student fill out another index card with name, address, phone number, birthday, and the last name of the person or persons he or she lives with at that address. This card is for your reference and for you to take home and use to make calls to students and students' families.

AFTER-LUNCH IDEA: Read aloud to the students. To follow up on the routine procedure of journal writing, begin reading journals written by famous people.

Planned Lessons and Activities (✤ ✦ ★ ✸)

Use the established cue to gain everyone's attention. The teacher begins to discuss and teach the need for consequences to support the classroom rules.

- **Topic**–Correction Plan

- **Opener**–Review the class rules, give examples of inappropriate behaviors, and have the students name the rule that is being broken.

- **Objectives**–The student will be able to

    1. List three reasons why correction is needed
    2. Describe the hierarchy of correction
    3. Create situations where correction is needed
    4. Plan a role-play using the correction plan

- **Instruction**–Discuss the need for a correction plan. Discuss the need for a hierarchy of consequences. Teach your correction plan. Go through the four steps (listed below), and demonstrate what it looks like to be reminded that a rule is not being followed. Inform the students that if something happens such as fighting, the teacher immediately jumps to step 4 and the student is removed from the classroom. Select a student to get help if such a situation develops in the classroom.

Below each step are suggested ways of carrying out the step. The teacher decides which suggestions to use and how many to offer in each category. The third and fourth steps must be consequences that the students don't like or they will take you to that level too often (see Figure 5.9 for a list of consequences). The correction plan is outlined below:

A. **Step 1–Nonverbal cues**

    1. Eye contact

    2. Proximity

    3. Body language

    4. Hand signal

B. **Step 2–Verbal cues**

    1. Use the student's name.

    2. Use an *I* statement such as "Billy, I need your attention now because I only have ten more minutes of class."

    3. Use words like *Stop, Check It*, or a word or phrase the students select to signal inappropriate behavior that must be stopped.

C. **Step 3–Time-out**

    1. Student goes to the assigned place in the room.

    2. Student goes to an assigned place in the room and writes in the behavior notebook what rule the student was not following and how to demonstrate more appropriate behavior in the future.

(✦) For middle school students, instead of time-out, call it *behavior redirection*. The student goes to another room and completes a behavior redirection sheet:

FIGURE 5.9 *List of Consequences*

1. Add time after school—alternate this duty with another teacher.

2. Take away free time—alternate with another teacher: one teacher takes students displaying appropriate behavior outside or to her room for fun or free time and the other teacher keeps the students displaying inappropriate behavior to finish an assignment or a consequence assignment.

3. Call for a conference—teacher and student or teacher, student, and parent or guardian.

4. Restrict Freedom Fridays.

5. Develop contracts for improving behavior.

6. Use checks, points, or demerits.

7. Give detention.

8. Issue conduct notices.

9. Send to principal.

10. Send to the counselor.

11. Call parents or guardians.

What happened? What did you do? Why was your action not the best choice? How would you respond to a similar situation in the future?

> 3. Student goes to the designated place out of the room, such as another classroom.

You can use colored index cards to work with the time-out procedure. For example, present a colored index card to the student. The color will convey the message and the procedure to follow. A green card means go to the designated time-out spot in the room for ten minutes and write in the behavior notebook—name, date, rule student broke, what student learned, and what student will do next time—and then the student returns to his or her seat. A yellow card means go to the designated time-out spot in the room, write in the behavior notebook, and then leave the classroom to work in another teacher's room (prearranged) for ten to fifteen minutes. A pink card indicates a conduct notice. The student must go to the teacher's desk, sit in the teacher's chair, write in the behavior notebook, write a letter home to parents or guardians explaining the conduct notice, and wait for the teacher to discuss the behavior with him or her before rejoining the class and returning to his or her seat.

D. **Step 4–Consequences**

1. In-class loss of free time, class detention, after-school time

2. Conduct notice

3. Call to parent or guardian

4. Conference with student, conference with student and parent or guardian

5. Trip to the principal

6. School detention, in-school suspension, suspension

- **Guided Practice**–Break the class into groups and let the students create situations where a correction plan would be needed using the steps above. The students must plan role-plays of the situations. Post the correction plan on the front wall.

- **Assessment**–Cruise (walk around the room), allow for questions and answers, and have students demonstrate the use of colored cards.

- **Closure**–Why does a teacher need a correction plan?

Why does a student need a correction plan? Does everyone understand the correction plan and the steps I will be using? Indicate with a thumbs up. (Teacher scans the room to see that all respond.)

Planned Lessons and Activities

Use the established cue to gain everyone's attention. This planned lesson continues as outlined in day 1 until everyone has been in the spotlight.

- **Topic**–Continue with Get to Know Your Classmates

- **Opener**–Begin by reviewing the names of students previously spotlighted by having those students stand up at the beginning of the activity. Quiz the class to see if they can remember their names and something about them.

- **Objectives**–The student will be able to

1. Review names and remember something about the students previously spotlighted
2. Name and learn something about two, four, or six new classmates

- **Instruction**–Ask the students if they know everyone in the class. Ask a student to name as many of the students as possible. Discuss why it is important to know each other in the class. Then ask the students to take out a piece of paper and fold it in half, twice, or three times to make two, four, or six squares.

- **Guided Practice**–Explain that for this activity they will have about twenty minutes to choose two, four, or six students to get to know. They are to write in each square of the paper a student's first name and one or two things about that student. Students must try to tell different things about themselves each time they are asked a question. Tell them you will blow a whistle when it is time to switch and then everyone must find someone else and begin again.

- **Assessment**–After the students have filled the squares, randomly or selectively choose two or four students to get to know and call out one name at a time. The students who have information on these students share it with the group. Listen to their responses.

- **Closure**–Ask students why it's important to know people in the class. Ask them to name one of the friends they learned about and tell something about that student.

END-OF-THE-DAY ROUTINE: Say to the students, "Tell me one thing you learned about how this class operates?"

GUIDELINES: Plan a show and tell activity. The younger students can bring in something you designate (something small, the next week something red, etc.) to place in a box. Older students can bring in trivia: They can write quotes, riddles, or brain teasers on strips of paper or cut out cartoons from newspapers or magazines and fold and place them in the *Funny* box. Each day a different student can select something out of the Funny box and share it with the class. Another box called *What's Up?* might be used for news clippings on current events to be collected and read or discussed.

REMINDERS:

- ✓ Get index cards (green, yellow, and pink).
- ✓ Assess students' learning needs.
- ✓ Prepare class schedules.

Day 3—Be Enthusiastic

BEGIN THE DAY: Greet students at the door. Say something specific to each student, such as, "Good Morning, you have your favorite color on today," or to another student, "Did you play baseball yesterday?" You can gather this personal information from the student responses to the get-acquainted activities (see Figures 5.3–5.6).

OPENING ACTIVITIES: Place reminders on the board for the students to follow:

1. Get your name tags.

2. Get ready for class.

3. Sit in your seat.

4. Be prepared for the Pledge of Allegiance and a silent moment.

ROUTINE PROCEDURE AND ACTIVITY TO BEGIN EACH DAY: The morning routine procedure is for students to get ready for class upon entering the room and to write in their journals. Monitor the routine procedure and give feedback.

USE CUE: Raise your hand and move to the front of the room. Get everyone's attention before beginning the lesson. Use strong and direct eye contact for compliance. Add names to the compliance expectation by saying, "John, I need your attention now," or "Mary, do you see the cue? Please, stop talking now." Time the students to see how long it takes to get everyone's attention. Share the results and challenge them to reduce the time.

GUIDELINES: Discuss the teacher's goal for how to begin. Describe progress with the morning routine procedure and activity. Give students information such as "Fifteen students were following the procedures when I scanned the room. That means 50 percent of you are really catching on to the process. Let's get 100 percent tomorrow." Develop a class expectation and goal for how to begin class. Discuss the need for other procedures. Begin to think in terms of developing class norms that are appropriate.

Discuss the use of the cue and tell the students how long it takes to get everyone's attention. Tell students what is reasonable and that additional time spent on getting everyone's attention will be taken off of students' time. "If you abuse it, you lose it," or "If you can handle it, you can have it." Time can be given and time can be taken. Make students aware you will be timing them for compliance. If acceptable, the class will receive a reward; if unacceptable, time will be taken from students.

OPENING ACTIVITIES: Explain to the class the method of taking attendance. The students will check themselves in each morning as they walk into the room. The teacher makes an attendance board with either magnetic name cards or name cards on clips. Lunch count can be taken at the same time. Include lunch cards or clips that say Choice #1 or Choice #2. Older students can be given a password and that is used to mark a class sign-in sheet. The teacher can use and mark a class roster when homework questions are asked of students. The teacher or attendance monitor can take the roll while the students are completing their opening activities.

ACTIVITY: Give each student a map of the school with special areas identified, such as school office, principal's office, nurse's station, restrooms, cafeteria, and auditorium. You can fill in these areas, or you can have the students fill in the special areas once they have located them. This activity is especially important to younger students and students coming to a new school. Returning students may want to record last year's teacher and mark that room, along with this year's teacher and their new room. An arrow line showing the fire drill route will be on the map. Students will discuss the route and mark and trace it. Post one map in the room and have the students place their maps in their orientation folders. Make sure you have enough copies to give to new students as they join the class throughout the year to help them feel more secure in a new place. Some learners may need a very basic map and will need help completing it. They may want to color it. The map can be laminated for the student's pocket or folder. The teacher may want to plan a tour of the school.

(♦) **Sixth-grade students definitely need a tour of the school if moving to a middle school. Groups of students can be assigned a peer to act as a tour guide.**

(♣) **Special populations need to take a tour of the school to become familiar with their surroundings. Each year, a tour is necessary to reacquaint them once again to the school.**

Planned Lessons and Activities

Use the established cue to gain everyone's attention. Teach one or two classroom rules a day until all rules have been taught. Remember to have discussions with the students that help them apply the rules to many different situations. Talk about the rules as they apply or overlap with situations outside of school or the classroom. For example, connect the rules to real life, such as at home, at work, at parties, or with friends.

- **Opener**–Use yesterday's assignment (the students were to look for two examples of respect) to discuss that rule briefly. Then introduce the next rule.

  Remember, rules should be taught from prepared lesson plans that include the Topic, Opener, Objectives, Instruction, Guided Practice, Assessment, Closure, and Independent Practice.

GUIDELINES: Begin using the textbooks. Most of the information for the first week or two is usually review material. Establish what the students should do when they have finished their work.

AFTER-LUNCH IDEA: Begin to read journal entries written by many different people for different purposes (for example, Anne Frank's diary, war accounts, and reminiscences of senior citizens).

Planned Lessons and Activities

Use the established cue to gain everyone's attention. Continue to teach the correction plan and further explain and demonstrate it. Decide on the procedure for time-out.

- **Topic**–Continue with Correction Plan

- **Opener**–Review rules by providing examples of a rule not being followed. The student will have to name the rule being broken and give the steps to the correction plan.

- **Objectives**–The student will be able to
  1. Apply the steps of the correction plan when class rules are not followed
  2. Describe step 3 (time-out) of the correction plan
  3. Fill in the required information on a behavior notebook page

- **Instruction**–Discuss step 3 of the correction plan. What is time-out? Can you think when it's used in sports? What is a time-out (thinking) chair? What does it mean to go to your room? Why is a time-out period important? Have you ever needed a time-out? If anyone gets to step 3 you must write in the behavior notebook. It will be placed at the time-out location. Identify the time-out location and show students the behavior notebook. Ask for a summary of what happens if a student is sent to time-out.

Discuss with students the contents of the behavior notebook page. For specific students (nonwriters), provide an audio recorder. The page includes the following:

Name and date

What rule did you break? What did you learn?

What will you do next time?

If referred to the principal's office, the student may take the behavior notebook for the principal to see. The behavior notebook may be shared with parents or guardians. It also serves to document behavior and frequency of behavioral problems.

- **Guided Practice**–Provide an example of a student breaking a rule and demonstrate the steps up to the time-out step. Then give everyone a page from the behavior notebook and have students fill out the page for this student and sign their name. Discuss the process and find out if they had difficulties filling out the page.

- **Assessment**–Cruise the room to make sure the work is completed. Let the students *share* a few pages. Have a question-and-answer period and collect these papers.

- **Closure**–What does *time-out* mean? What step of the correction plan is time-out? In time-out, what questions are you to answer in the behavior notebook? Do you have to get to step 3? What can you do to stay away from time-out? What is step 1? What is step 2? What is step 4?

Use colored index cards to demonstrate step 3 (time-out procedure). Present a card to a student. The color indicates a procedure to be followed. In step 3, a green card means go to designated time-out spot in the room for ten minutes and write in the behavior notebook—name, date, rule student broke, what student learned, and what student will do next time—and then the student will return to his or her seat; a yellow card means go to the designated time-out spot in the room and write in the behavior notebook and then leave the classroom to work in another teacher's room (prearranged) for ten to fifteen minutes.

A pink card means a conduct notice and the student must go to the teacher's desk, sit in the teacher's chair, write in the behavior notebook, write a letter home to parents or guardians explaining the conduct notice, and wait for the teacher to discuss the behavior before rejoining the class and returning to his or her seat.

Planned Lessons and Activities

Use the established cue to gain everyone's attention. This planned lesson continues as outlined in day 1 until everyone has been in the spotlight.

- **Topic**–Continue with Get to Know Your Classmates

- **Opener**–Review the names of the students previously spotlighted by having those students stand up at the beginning of the activity and quizzing the class to see if they can remember their names and something about them.

- **Objectives**–The student will be able to

  1. Recall names and remember something about the students previously spotlighted
  2. Name and learn something about two, four, or six new classmates

ACTIVITY: Have students write something about themselves on index cards and personalize each card. Have them write their names on the backs of their cards, share them with the class, and put them on a bulletin board headlined "Who am I? Who are we?" The teacher should complete a card, too.

END-OF-THE-DAY ROUTINE: Say, "Tell me something that you learned as a ___ grader that you didn't know when you were in ___ grade."

GUIDELINES: Remind students to bring certain objects or cartoons, riddles, and quotes to school to put in the Funny box.

REMINDERS:

  ✓ Bring a stop watch or timer.
  ✓ Bring colored index cards.

✓ Prepare bulletin board.

✓ Cut out fifty hands (in white or colored paper) or have students trace hands and cut them out.

Day 4—Be Positive

BEGIN THE DAY: Greet the students at the door. Remember to voice specifics pertaining to each student.

OPENING ACTIVITIES: Put a reminder cloud or a list on the board for students to get name tags, take attendance, and be ready for class. The class will say or hear the Pledge of Allegiance and have a silent moment.

ROUTINE PROCEDURE: The morning routine procedure is for students to get ready for class upon entering the room and to write in their journals. The teacher monitors students and makes positive comments to them following the procedure. The teacher says, "I like the way you (name, names, groups, rows, etc.) came into class, finished all the readiness tasks, and started writing in your journal." Based on your observations, you may have to provide topics, questions, statements, for example, for their journal write.

(♣ ✳) For students who may not be able to write in their journals, they may be able to draw pictures or cut out pictures from magazines. If some students have goals of writing a limited number of sentences, when they are finished, they can be helpers and distribute and collect journals.

USE CUE: Raise your hand and move to the front of the room. Continue to use the cue and time the response. Report the time it took for attention to be focused on the teacher. If given a satisfactory response, reward the class. You may want to add time to an agreed upon incentive. If unsatisfactory, take that amount of time from an incentive. Establish an expectation that time gained is given to the students, but time wasted is time given to the teacher. "If you abuse it, you lose it." Provide a specific on how this will be done. The students may not need a reward or consequence; they may just enjoy beating the clock or working with the time. Discuss with the class how they can assist each other in following the beginning-of-class procedures.

ACTIVITY: Place the class schedule of times for subjects, specials (art, music, physical education, library), and lunch on the chalkboard and discuss it with students. Older students can copy the schedule and younger students receive a prepared schedule to include in the orientation folder. A class schedule will also be posted on the side wall. For special student populations, the schedule becomes a predictable occurrence in their school life.

GUIDELINES: Brainstorm and list jobs needed to make a class run smoothly. Review how attendance is taken. Discuss jobs such as line leader, lunch-ticket collector, board washer, office messenger, cafeteria-table washers, sweepers, and visitor monitor. Discuss the job descriptions. Assign the jobs to students and have them write their responsibilities on a sheet of paper. Review, discuss, and possibly revise the roles and responsibilities and have the students write them in their notebooks. Students are accepting and initiating "ownership" in the management of their class.

Also choose a student for the job of *peer assistant*, a student who will assist students with questions when the teacher is busy. Another job is the *class contact*, who helps new students become familiar with class. The *homework helper* records who has turned in the homework. The class may need more assigned jobs as the weeks progress. The teacher trains the helper or first group of class helpers. Each class helper selects and trains an assistant, who then assumes the responsibilities the following month. This means the teacher only trains the first set of helpers.

Make a bulletin board or poster titled "Helping Hands" to post jobs as needed and assign students to the jobs. Names for jobs may change as often as you like. Place both the job and the student's name on hands and put together on the bulletin board.

(✤) **Find appropriate class jobs for special education students to integrate them into the inclusion setting. If in the self-contained setting, assign jobs to them to provide some ownership of their classroom. Some of the tasks may include sorting, cleaning, running errands, and taking visitors to the classroom. Be watchful of class jobs because there may be some tasks the students are unable to do.**

Planned Lessons and Activities (✤ ✦ ✱)

Use the established cue to gain everyone's attention. Begin to teach the Personal Problem/Solution Plan:

- **Topic**–Personal Problem/Solution Plan

- **Opener**–Discuss with the students the kinds of behaviors that keep them from learning, concentrating, or feeling good about themselves.

- **Objectives**–The student will be able to

    1. Identify behaviors that interfere with learning
    2. List three reasons why he or she needs to handle problems
    3. Describe the personal problem/solution plan
    4. Demonstrate situations where the personal problem/solution plan would be needed

- **Instruction**–Discuss reasons why students need to handle problems or have a method to use in solving problems. Discuss times and instances when all of us might be bothered by the actions of another person (at the movies, in the cafeteria, on the playground). Teach the steps to the personal problem/solution plan (Bosch & Kersey, 1993, p. 229):

  1. First, try ignoring the person who is bothering you. (Put imaginary ear muffs over your ears.) If necessary, turn, look at, or if possible, move away from the person.
  2. If that doesn't work, ask the person politely to stop. "I cannot do my work when you are ____."
  3. If that doesn't work, tell the person in a loud voice to "Stop it," "Cut it out," or "I don't like that."
  4. If that doesn't work, ask the teacher if you can speak in private. (Student could be provided with a yellow card for this step.) Arrange a time to talk. Tell the teacher the problem and let him or her offer suggestions.
  5. If that doesn't work, ask the teacher if you can speak to the principal. Talk over the problem with the principal and ask for help in finding a permanent solution.

  (Reprinted with permission of the Helen Dwight Reid Educational Foundation. Published by Heldref Publications, 1319 18th Street, NW Washington, DC 20036-18020.)

- **Guided Practice**–Assign the students to groups and let them name situations in which the personal problem/solution plan would be needed. Then have them role-play the situations and the steps to the plan. Post the personal problem/solution plan.

- **Assessment**–Cruise the room and note student responses. Have a class roster form on a clipboard that lists the students' names and areas to be assessed. Check off if the students seem to understand the material. Clipboarding provides assessment documentation for many procedures and state standards of learning that may indicate mastery, proficiency, or areas to reteach, review, or remediate. You also can note the need for individual one-on-one instruction (such as working with the teacher, a paraeducator, volunteer, or parent or guardian). These assessments can be placed in file folders and labeled.

- **Closure**–Why do students need to have a personal problem/solution plan? Does everyone understand the steps to take when another person is interfering with your freedom to learn? Show a thumbs up, pat yourself on the back, or give your shoulder partner a high five.

AFTER-LUNCH IDEA: Teacher reads aloud from journals or books that are relevant to current topics of study.

Planned Lessons and Activities

Use the established cue to gain everyone's attention. This planned lesson continues as outlined in day 1 until everyone has been in the spotlight.

- **Topic**–Continue with Get to Know Your Classmates
- **Opener**–Review the names of the students previously spotlighted by having them stand up at the beginning of the activity. Quiz the class to see if they can remember their names and something about them.
- **Objectives**–The student will be able to
  1. Recall names and remember something about the students spotlighted
  2. Name and learn something about two, four, or six new classmates

END-OF-THE-DAY ROUTINE: Ask students, "How will rules help you in this classroom? How do they help you at home? How do they help you in a work environment? Why do we say that rules can allow and not restrict?"

Review the index cards with examples of respect the students wrote in a previous lesson.

GUIDELINES: Select a student greeter to join you at the door in the mornings for the week. Post the student greeter's name on the front board. Remind students to bring certain objects or cartoons, riddles, and quotes to school and put them in the Funny box or news clippings of current events for the What's Up? box.

REMINDER:

- ✓ Prepare card box (birthday cards, special occasions).

Second Week

Second Week Goal: Review, Monitor, and Reteach What Is Important

Key Teaching Areas

- ❏ Review management plan.
- ❏ Review rules and procedures.
- ❏ Review correction plan and personal problem/solution plan (PPSP).
- ❏ Develop and teach incentives.
- ❏ Increase student accountability.

Strategies for Success

- ❏ Get the parents or guardians involved.
- ❏ Provide get-acquainted activities.
- ❏ Use positive ripple effect.
- ❏ Use catch-them-being-good strategy.
- ❏ Provide praise, rewards, feedback, and encouragement.

Self-Reflective Opportunities

- ❏ Maintain a daily or weekly electronic journal. Add reflections at the end of the day or week, which may showcase teaching highlights and stumbling blocks. Make a list of those students needing encouragement.
- ❏ Contact other first-year teachers from your list of contacts and share your experiences with them.

REMINDERS:

- ✓ Plain index cards
- ✓ Buddy card box

Day 1—Smile

BEGIN THE DAY: Teacher and student greeter meet the students in the morning. Connect with the students by saying some things you remember about them.

OPENING ACTIVITIES: Place the reminder cloud or a list on the board to remind students to get name tags, take attendance, and be ready for class. Have the class recite the Pledge of Allegiance and have a silent moment. Have students remove the name cards from the bulletin board and collect them. (The cards will be used in day 2 of the second week.)

ROUTINE PROCEDURE: The morning routine procedure is for students to get ready for class upon entering the room and to write in their journals. Monitor this procedure and correct behavior that is inappropriate.

USE CUE: Raise your hand and move to the front of the room. Time how long it takes for everyone's attention. Report or record the time and comment on the amount of assistance students offered to each other. Suggest that *buddies* help each other. Be consistent in following the process: if satisfactory, reward class; if unsatisfactory, take time away.

ACTIVITY: Assign a buddy to each student. Buddies can change after each grading period or four times a year. Explain to the students why this is important. Use

Think-Pair-Share for the following activity. Let the student buddies get into pairs for approximately five minutes and have each pair develop a procedure for being a school buddy. They will write down this information along with their buddies' address, telephone number, and birthday. Use the think aloud strategy and let the students share their procedures for all to hear. How many are the same? How many are different? Do you need to change your procedure or add something to your procedure? The responsibilities that need to be discussed thoroughly are what to do if a buddy is absent, has an extended illness, or is celebrating a birthday. For example, the buddy is responsible for getting an appropriate birthday or get-well card from the card box to send to his or her buddy. Buddies can plan special events and share special news about their buddies. For special student populations, care must be taken to pair students with appropriate others. Students need to rotate being a special population partner.

Think-Pair-Share activities are a great way to begin developing cooperative learning. Start with small groups (pairs) and begin developing the skills needed to work in larger groups and for different purposes. The Think-Pair-Share strategy is quick, usually successful, and can be used anytime. It is especially valuable when a teacher experiences a lack of student participation, energy, or interest. For example, ask pairs to summarize the lesson so far, formulate some questions about the material, list advantages of a concept, or tell why certain information is important to learn. The teacher must be able to move from whole group to small group instruction as often as needed to keep students engaged in the learning process and focused on the content.

(♣ ✳) When special learners are in groups, assign specific tasks to each person so all members feel like they are contributing to the whole.

A nonverbal cue or code for forming different group arrangements from pairs to groups of three and four is essential. A hand code may be taught to signal the students to get into different group arrangements. Holding up two fingers could indicate a Think-Pair-Share activity, three fingers a group of three, four fingers a group of four (cooperative learning), index finger a special grouping in which the students are assigned to the group based on ability, and the thumb could be a special group based on student choices of teammates. A hand raised with all five fingers extended may indicate stop and all eyes focus on the teacher for further instructions. Remember the signals must be taught and the students must practice forming groups quickly on cue before group learning assignments can be made.

GUIDELINES: Review bulletin board or poster of class jobs. Quiz students on jobs and tasks. Also review the classroom management plan (review rules and procedures, correction plan, and PPSP).

Planned Lessons and Activities (✤ ✦ ★ ✳)

Use the established cue to gain everyone's attention. Begin to develop and teach incentives to support the classroom rules.

- **Topic**–Incentive Plan

- **Opener**–Ask students what incentives and rewards mean to them. What is your favorite reward? When is a reward given to you? Why is it given?

- **Objectives**–The student will be able to

  1. Identify rewards for appropriate behavior
  2. Examine situations when rewards are given
  3. Choose three to five rewards to be used in this class

- **Instruction**–Discuss with students possible incentives for appropriate behavior and academic achievement. Brainstorm ideas for individual and group rewards that a teacher can use in a classroom. Write their ideas on the board under two categories: Individual Rewards and Class Rewards. Discuss the ideas and the situations in which they could be applied. Have the students choose three to five incentives for the class. Keep a list so that different rewards may be earned from time to time or as effectiveness diminishes.

- **Guided Practice**–Present situations and have students decide whether a reward is warranted. Discuss and explain your expectations.

- **Assessment**–"Cruise, question, and answer" and "check for understanding" to get a quick snapshot of the whole class to determine their understanding of the material. The check for understanding should show a majority. Examples of checks for understanding are as follows:

Provide a question, statement, scenario, example and

- Ask for agree or disagree

- Ask for a thumbs up, down, or sideways

- Ask for a stand up

- Ask for a vote on a selection, choice, or response

- Ask for a summary (can be by individual, pair, table top, row, or group)

- Ask for a *Quick Write* and share (can be by individual, pair, table top, row, or group); a Quick Write is giving students one to five minutes to summarize (in writing) what they have learned so far. Students then read from their written notes.

- Ask for a *think-a-minute* (can be by individual, pair, table top, row, or group). A think-a-minute is an opportunity for students to provide an oral response to a question(s) posed by the teacher. The teacher gives one to three minutes of silence for the students to think about the question(s), followed by discussion.

For this lesson: The check for understanding strategy is to provide a scenario and place three options (responses) on the board. Students select A, B, or C as the correct answer. Tally the responses or watch if you ask them to stand up if they responded with A, then, B, and then, C. If they look around at others to see what they are doing, they are unsure learners. Repeat examples or reteach areas before assigning independent practice.

- **Closure**–Why are rewards important?

- **Independent Practice**–Write the rewards on the board. Have older students copy them and place the copy in their orientation folder. Pass out a reward. Have younger students draw a picture of the reward they like best. Pass out stickers to each student. (See Figure 5.10 for list of incentives.)

AFTER-LUNCH IDEA: Read aloud to students.

Planned Lessons and Activities

Use the established cue to gain everyone's attention. This planned lesson continues as outlined in day 1 until everyone has been in the spotlight.

- **Topic**–Continue with Get to Know Your Classmates

- **Opener**–Review the names of the students previously spotlighted by having them stand at the beginning of the activity. Quiz the class to see if they can remember their names and something about them.

- **Objectives**–The student will be able to

    1. Recall names and something about the students spotlighted
    2. Name and learn something about two, four, or six new classmates

END-OF-THE-DAY ROUTINE: Review the rules. Students need to memorize rules and understand that rules have a purpose in their classroom. The students will complete the following three sentences.

1. The rule that makes the most sense to me is _____.

2. The rule I might change is _____.

3. Rules help me when _____.

FIGURE 5.10   *List of Incentives*

1. Homework passes	8. Center time
2. Treasure box	9. Token economies
3. Recognition reinforcers	10. Auctions
4. Ice cream, candies	11. Points
5. Freedom Fridays	12. Preferred activity time
6. Parties	13. Catch-them-being-good notes
7. Talk time	14. Marble jar

Collect this assignment and place it in the orientation folders. For younger students, take one sentence, discuss it, write it the way they want to complete it, and read it together or copy it.

GUIDELINES: Inform the students that you are going to start calling parents and guardians to introduce yourself to them starting this evening and each night this week until all are called. Have them tell their mom, dad, or guardian that you will be calling this week to say hello.

REMINDERS:

✓ Begin calling about five parents or guardians each night to say hello and give the date of the open house. Ask for their support for a great year. Let them know you are available and need their input to be truly effective. Record the dates of the calls and other information on student index cards. Be sure these are positive calls to parents or guardians and you say something positive— something that you know and like about the student—when conversing with that parent or guardian. This is another one of those first impressions that must set you apart from some of the other teachers, especially those teachers whose first call to the student's home is to report problems. Most parents or guardians associate a call from the teacher with bad news.

✓ Get colored index cards.

✓ Make class roster forms for student helpers to record homework and other tasks.

✓ Prepare an assignment sheet.

✓ Prepare a calendar.

✓ Collect name cards.

✓ Prepare *Get Off* forms.

Day 2—Be Realistic: You Can't Divide Yourself Into Twenty-Six Pieces

BEGIN THE DAY: Teacher and student greeter meet the students in the morning.

OPENING ACTIVITIES: Put a reminder cloud or a list on the board to remind students to take attendance, be ready for class, and begin the routine procedure. The class will recite the Pledge of Allegiance and have a silent moment.

ROUTINE PROCEDURE: The morning routine procedure is for the students to get ready for class upon entering the room and to write in their journals. Monitor this procedure. Ask successful students to provide information on how they get prepared. Have one or two students summarize this information in steps. For example, what they do first, second, and last. Ask if everyone understands thumbs up or any other signal you choose, scan the room, and move on to the next thing.

USE CUE: Raise your hand and move to the front of the room. Continue to monitor amount of time it takes to get everyone's attention.

OPENING ACTIVITIES: Shuffle and pass out the personalized name cards collected previously. A student will stand up and show the back side of the card, which has his or her name on it. The class will agree or disagree that the name matches the person who was dealt the card. If the students say it's a match and they are correct, the student can place the card back on the bulletin board. If it is not a match, the student must find the correct person, and the class will again agree or disagree with the match. If a match is made, the student puts the card back on the bulletin board. Once this activity is completed, the name cards remain on the bulletin board.

GUIDELINES (✦ ★): Prepare an assignment sheet to be used by the students to alert them to topics or concepts that will be taught, the amount of information to be covered, and the requirements and due dates for completed assignments. This will enable the student to plan ahead and possibly plan to do the assignments at more convenient times. Explain how each student is held accountable through this assignment sheet and can make appropriate decisions based on his or her needs and time constraints.

Make it clear that homework assignments not completed at home will be completed during the school day. Share a philosophy statement, "I accept no excuses. I just expect action." Give them an example: "If a student comes into the classroom without the homework, what is my expectation? My expectation is that the student must do something about an assignment that isn't completed by the time it is due." The student may have to build in time during the school day for unfinished work as well as fun.

Establish a specific day, such as the first Monday of the month, to pass out assignment sheets. Draw students' attention to information on the sheet. Make sure they know the importance of the assignment sheet and your expectations for its use. When students focus on the assignment sheet, it gives the work a higher priority and sends a message that this is important. The assignment sheet can be prepared weekly or monthly.

For younger students, prepare a weekly or monthly calendar. Fill in some class-specific information, such as dates of speakers, field trips, and special classes (e.g., art, physical education, and music). The student can fill in other information as it is presented. The younger students can fill in a limited amount of information and color or put stickers on key events, dates, birthdays of classmates, and so on. The birthday information should come from the buddy. Remind the buddies of their responsibilities.

An assignment sheet, calendar, or both should be included in the orientation folder to alert the parents or guardians that this information will be coming home at a certain time (establish a day). With students and parents or guardians well informed, you can have high expectations for students' learning and parental support.

AFTER-LUNCH IDEA: Read aloud to students.

Planned Lessons and Activities (✤ ✦ ★ ✳)

Use the established cue to gain everyone's attention. Begin to teach specific rewards and techniques. You may choose to teach one, two, or possibly all of these techniques.

- **Topic**–*Marble jar, Secret Word, Get Off form*, and *Catch-Them-Being-Good Technique.* (Omit the Get Off form for the younger students.)

- **Opener**–Show the students a jar. Catch someone being good and drop a few marbles in the jar. Next, catch the class doing something good and drop a few more marbles in the jar. Ask students what they think about this marble jar. If you're using Secret Word, you can introduce this technique by playing the game Hangman.

- **Objectives**–The student will be able to

    1. Explain the use of the marble jar, Secret Word, and the Get Off form
    2. Recognize the catch-them-being-good technique

- **Instruction**–Begin by telling the students about the marble jar and its purpose. Give specific examples of how to earn marbles.

    Discuss Secret Word. The class decides on a positive reward for using appropriate behavior. When you note good behavior, write the first letter of the reward on the chalkboard. When the word is spelled, the students receive the reward. Explain that you will "catch them being good" when rules and procedures are followed; when they respond immediately to your cue; when students are kind, considerate, and helpful to one another; or giving 100 percent to a situation. Remind them the rewards they choose must be realistic and practical. Tell them that once the marble jar is filled or the secret word is spelled, the reward is given, and we start again with an empty marble jar or another word.

- **Guided Practice**–Have students write down possible class rewards on slips of paper and collect the slips.

- **Assessment**–The teacher will tally the responses and announce the class reward the next day.

- **Instruction**–The teacher explains the Get Off form. This form is a reward that is given to a student who is caught being good. The form entitles the student to get out of an assignment. For example, the student may use the form to get out of homework or an in-class assignment by simply turning it in to you in place of the assignment. The student may save the forms to use at a later date; however, only one form can be turned in on a single day.

- **Guided Practice**–Have the students summarize the procedure on how to use the Get Off form.

- **Assessment**–Listen to summarizations.

- **Closure**–What is the purpose of the marble jar? How many think we will be able to fill this jar? What is the Secret-Word technique? How many of you plan to get a Get Off form? Explain the catch-them-being-good technique?

- **Independent Practice**–Have students write a paragraph or verbally explain the marble jar, Secret Word, Get Off form, and catch-them-being-good technique. If students write a paragraph, place it in their orientation folders.

END-OF-THE-DAY ROUTINE: Use a concept-webbing idea to review the day's learning. Make sure the correction plan is reviewed at this time.

GUIDELINES: Remind the students you are going to call different parents or guardians each night until you have introduced yourself to all the parents or guardians. Tell them to tell their mom, dad, or guardian that you will be calling this week to say hello. They should expect your call. Remember to call from school and not provide your home phone or caller ID number. If parents or guardians do not have a phone, please provide a personal note for the student to take home to share with mom, dad, or guardian.

REMINDERS:

- ✓ Prepare and reproduce contract form.
- ✓ Remember Funny box or What's Up? box.

✓ Bring cans.

✓ Continue to call about five parents or guardians each night to say hello, give them the date of the open house, and ask for their support for a great year. Let them know you are available and need their input to be truly effective.

Day 3—Be Flexible

BEGIN THE DAY: Teacher and student greeter meet the students in the morning. Remember to smile and say something positive.

OPENING ACTIVITIES: Put the reminder cloud or a list on the board to remind students to take attendance, prepare for class, and begin the routine procedure. The class will recite the Pledge of Allegiance and have a silent moment.

ROUTINE PROCEDURE: The morning routine procedure is for the students to get ready for class upon entering the room and to write in their journals. Continue to monitor. If the majority follows the procedure appropriately, then reteaching is not necessary. If a few students are having difficulty with the routine procedure, reteach it to them and give an incentive to the majority as a reward. You must reinforce what you expect and what you require.

USE CUE: Raise your hand and move to the front of the room.

GUIDELINES: Have students complete their first writing sample to be placed in a performance portfolio by completing these sentences: I can . . . , I'm proud of . . . , Last year I learned . . . , This year I want to learn . . . , for example. The sentence completion activity is appropriate for all learners. The teacher can assist the younger students by writing their responses down or helping them write their responses. You can add more or more complex sentences if you are working with an advanced class or a higher grade level.

(✦ ★) An alternative to the sentence completion is to write a paragraph or story from an uncompleted sentence. List two or three sentences from which each student can select one to begin the paragraph or story.

The performance portfolio consists of a large folder for each student that is placed in a key location in the classroom. The portfolios represent the work students do as they progress through the school year. The students can evaluate their own progress.

For the elementary grades, the teacher can collect soup cans, remove the labels, and distribute them to the students. The students will be instructed to decorate their cans. Each time a student masters something, he or she writes it down on a piece of paper (or the teacher writes it down), rolls up the paper, ties a string around it, and places it in the can. Once a month, the student takes the can home to share the good news with parents or guardians.

AFTER-LUNCH IDEA: Read aloud to students.

GUIDELINES: During an activity from the day before, the students were asked to write down possible group rewards that they would like when the marble jar is filled or the secret word is completed. Announce the reward chosen by the majority.

Planned Lessons and Activities (✤ ✦ ★)

Use the established cue to gain everyone's attention. Continue with the incentive part of the correction plan by introducing contracts.

- **Topic**–Contracts

- **Opener**–If you were a teacher, what would you do if you saw that one student did not need to do as many math problems as most of the class? What would you do if you saw that some students simply could not do all the work assigned because they work at a slower pace, but yet they understand the process? These students would be receiving a grade of F or Incomplete. Does this really tell you what they can do and what they know?

- **Objectives**–The student will be able to

  1. Describe the use of contracts in this classroom
  2. Explain the contract procedure

- **Instruction**–Lead the students in a discussion of solutions to meet learning needs. List the solutions on the board. If contracts are not a part of the discussion, you must introduce this concept. Teach them how contracts will be used in the classroom. The contracts are for three distinct purposes: learning differences, enrichment opportunities, and changing behavior. Provide examples of use in the three areas. Ask the students for examples. Explain the contract procedure and that you will be making these decisions based on student needs. Tell the students this is a teacher decision and is not open to discussion. Remind them that everyone will be under contract at some time during the year, maybe more than once. Much of the recording and monitoring of contracts is done with forms and checklists, which a student helper or parent or guardian volunteer can do. The contract is initially drawn up between a student and teacher for a set period of time and discussed thoroughly. Put the contract in a file folder for ease in recording information on the inside of the folder.

- **Guided Practice**–Have each student fill out a contract and the necessary forms. Use the smart board to highlight the form and information. Have the students sign and date the form and place it in the performance portfolios. (A sample contract can be seen in Figure 5.11.)

FIGURE 5.11   *Sample Contract*

The Contract

Student's Name _____

Teacher's Name _____

Parent or Guardian's Name _____

Date _____

Contract Purpose: _____

_____

_____

_____

The teacher promises to _____

_____

_____

The student promises to _____

_____

_____

The parent or guardian promises to _____

_____

_____

My goal is to _____

_____

_____

_____

- **Assessment**–Scan and Cruise

- **Closure**–What are contracts? Why are they important? What are the three uses of contracts in this classroom? Give me some information on the contract procedure?

END-OF-THE-DAY ROUTINE: Ask students what choice has to do with the correction plan. The student can choose to change inappropriate to appropriate behavior before you direct a behavior change through consequences (steps 3 and 4). You can use the Think-Pair-Share activities during closure.

GUIDELINES: Remind the students you are going to call parents or guardians each night until you have introduced yourself to all the parents and guardians. Tell them to tell their mom, dad, or guardian that you will be calling this week to say hello.

REMINDERS:

- ✓ Remember the Funny box or What's Up? box.

- ✓ Remember the marble jar.

- ✓ Remember index cards.

- ✓ Prepare strips of paper.

- ✓ Continue to call about five parents or guardians each night to say hello and give them the date of the open house and to ask for their support for a great year.

- ✓ Prepare contract management plans.

Day 4—Have a Sense of Humor

BEGIN THE DAY: Teacher and student greeter meet the students in the morning.

OPENING ACTIVITIES: Place the reminder cloud or a list on the board to remind students to take attendance, be ready for class, and begin the routine procedure. The class will recite the Pledge of Allegiance and have a silent moment.

ROUTINE PROCEDURE: The morning routine procedure is for the students to get ready for class upon entering the room and to write in their journals.

USE CUE: Raise your hand and move to the front of the room. Continue to monitor the amount of time it takes to get everyone's attention. If the students take too much time, take time from them to reinforce this procedure.

GUIDELINES (❖ ✦ ★ ✳): The class will have the opportunity to ask questions about the management plan. For younger students, see how much they have memorized.

For older students, review the management plan by putting it into outline form or steps. The teacher may want to place the plan on the board or smart board and leave blanks for missing information. The students could come to the front of the room and fill in the missing information and place their initials after the supplied text. Follow this progression of concepts: rules, teacher's expectations, correction plan steps, teacher's expectations, and incentives. Discuss the role of the student and the role of the teacher to ensure a positive learning environment that maximizes learning potential and minimizes disruptions.

You should have prepared a contract of the management plan that includes the class rules, correction plan, consequences, incentives, and rewards. The student should read it carefully before signing the contract. At the bottom of the contract, the student signs the statement, "I, (name), agree to abide by this contract management plan."

The students are to take their orientation folders home and discuss the folder and contract with their parents or guardians as a homework assignment. The contract should be returned the next day with their parent's or guardian's signature. Offer a reward for "next day delivery" of the signed contracts. After you receive the signed contract, make two additional copies. The copies are for the parents or guardians, teacher, and student.

AFTER-LUNCH IDEA: Read aloud to students.

Planned Lessons and Activities (♣ ♦ ★ ✳)

Use the established cue to gain everyone's attention. The teacher continues to prepare students to work together and learn together.

- **Topic**–Cooperative Learning

- **Opener**–Discuss the saying, "Two heads are better than one." This class is going to work together and learn together.

- **Objectives**–The student will be able to

    1. List three advantages of cooperative learning
    2. Discuss three disadvantages of cooperative learning
    3. Propose solutions to the disadvantages

- **Instruction**–Demonstrate cooperative learning by giving one student a list of three words and a dictionary. Pick three more students and give them the same list of three words and three dictionaries. Tell the class that these three will work together and the other student will work alone. They must look up the words and write on a piece of paper the page number found or phonetic spelling and the first definition. Give them a signal to begin. While this is being done, ask the other students, "Who do you think will finish first? Why?" Ask the participants how they liked working in a team. Have the class focus on the word *cooperation*. Brainstorm three advantages of cooperative learning. Discuss possible disadvantages and solutions. Place information on the board in three columns: Advantages, Disadvantages, Solutions. Have students take notes.

- **Assessment**–*Monitor* to make sure students are taking notes and *mentor* to add encouragement. Place these notes in the orientation folder.

- **Closure**–What do you think is the greatest advantage of cooperative learning or working together? What does cooperation mean to you?

END-OF-THE-DAY ROUTINE: Say to students, "Give me a situation where the personal problem/solution plan might be needed."

A closure game is a fun way to review for tomorrow, the last day of the week. You can review the classroom management plan and subject content. Write the concepts you've taught on strips of paper. Have students select a strip and tell something about it.

GUIDELINES: Establish a procedure for turning in homework and create a homework recording form. Identify the place to put homework and remind the homework helper to collect and record completed homework on the form. The homework recording form is placed in the Teacher basket first thing in the morning. The contract is the first official homework.

Remind the students you are going to call parents and guardians each night until all have been called.

REMINDERS:

- ✓ Remember Funny box or What's Up? box.
- ✓ Remember marble jar.
- ✓ Bring ingredients for making a meat and cheese sandwich.
- ✓ Continue to call about five parents or guardians each night to say hello, give them the date of the open house, and ask for their support for a great year. Let them know you are available and need their input to be truly effective.

Day 5—TGIF

BEGIN THE DAY: Teacher and student greeter meet the students in the morning.

OPENING ACTIVITIES: Place a reminder cloud or a list on the board or a poster for students to put homework in the Homework basket. The student assigned to check homework assignments must record information on the Homework form and place it in the Teacher basket.

ROUTINE PROCEDURE: The morning routine procedure is for students to be ready for class upon entering the room and to write in their journals. Continue to monitor and reward if possible.

USE CUE: Raise your hand and move to the front of the room.

GUIDELINES: Report the number of students turning in the first homework assignment—the contract—on the due day and how many still must turn in their homework assignments. Discuss the homework policy. Share your expectations for the homework assignments. Discuss the importance of homework. Tell them your teaching style is not to give a failing grade or an incomplete or a grade of F to anyone, but to make sure the work assigned is understood and completed. Review the homework policy again and repeat that time will be provided for those students who have not finished their homework. Those students who have completed their work will be given an incentive or a fun time activity. The students will review this procedure by performing the following role-play described below:

Student: "Mrs. James, I don't have my homework. I left it on the bus."

Teacher: "Okay, what can you do about this?"

Student: "I can do it now before class, at the scheduled time during the day, or if I finish today's work."

Teacher: "Which one are you going to do?"

Student: "I'm going to do it right now."

To support the homework policy, select two days a week to assign homework. Inform the parents or guardians of the two days that homework will be assigned. Give interesting homework assignments and use creative approaches: ask students to complete all the odd-numbered problems, the first five, the last five, or boys do even, girls do odd; and possibly, add choice by giving two assignments and allowing the students to choose one. *Middle school and secondary students* usually have homework for every class. *Middle school teachers* have commented that if the homework is started in class, the percentage of completed homework received the next day increases.

AFTER-LUNCH IDEA: Read aloud to students.

Planned Lessons and Activities (✤ ✦ ★ ✳)

Use the established cue to gain everyone's attention. Continue to promote cooperative learning. Support the process with a specific procedure to follow:

- **Topic**–Guidelines for Giving Directions

- **Opener**–What are some of your favorite things to eat? How do you make a cake? Who assembled your bike? How do you write a research paper? Everyone needs directions. Sometimes directions are difficult to understand. Directions in this class are made simpler through a procedure. Let's learn the procedure.

- **Objectives**–The student will be able to

  1. Examine the importance of understanding directions
  2. Describe the procedure for giving directions

- **Instruction**–Ask the students, "What are some ways directions can be improved?" Have students come to the board and write their answers. Have the students pass the marker to the next person who comes to the board. Write the students' ideas on the board. Pass out index cards and ask each student to write directions for making a meat and cheese sandwich. Collect the cards. Select a card and have a student read the first direction, pass the card to another student to read the second direction, and continue until all directions have been read. Demonstrate making the sandwich by following their directions. The students will begin to see the need for directions to be clear, specific, and given in an ordered way. Introduce the *Guidelines for Giving Directions* that will be used in this classroom. Use a poster or smart board to display the list of steps (see below). Describe the steps in detail.

The direction-giving procedure includes the following (Bosch, 1991):

1. ***Provide specific and simply stated directions.***
   a. Break down directions into steps.
   b. If there are more than three steps, put directions on a poster, smart board, or handout for the students to refer to during the task.

2. ***Teach the steps one at a time.***
   a. Use discussions, explanations, and examples.
   b. Use the "give and get" process—the teacher gives directions and gets the directions back from the students before moving to the next step.

3. ***Establish a cue that tells the students to stop and shift attention to the teacher.***

4. ***Set a time limit for the assignment.***

5. ***Inform the students of the evaluation (turned in, graded, exchanged papers, or discussed).***
   a. Use an individual assignment.
   b. Use a group assignment.

6. ***Ask if there are any questions. Tell students if they don't understand, they must ask questions now. Questions will not be taken after this time.***

7. *Last step: If the students will be working in groups, assign members and pass out work. Greatest mistake is distributing the worksheets before giving the directions and the same for forming groups. A direction-giving procedure comes first or the teacher loses the students' attention.*

8. *Give students time to begin their work independently before monitoring their work.*

Place a poster of the Guidelines for Giving Directions on the wall. The students will be able to follow the steps while you are giving directions. You will use the steps each time you give directions for individual assignments and cooperative learning activities. The most important steps are the "give and get" step and the step asking if there are any questions. Remember, when you have gone through the steps and students have started the activity and they have questions, stop the activity and return to the steps emphasizing when to ask questions. Then say, "Now, are we ready to begin?" You must teach, stop, and reteach the procedure to make it work and to increase and maintain students' accountability to the direction-giving procedure.

- **Assessment**–Question and Answer
- **Closure**–Why are directions important? How am I going to give directions to you? How can you make sure you understand the directions?

  (Reprinted with permission. Published by National Middle School Association. Copyright 1991.)

END-OF-THE-DAY ROUTINE: Use the closure game you prepared for review. Have students select a strip on which you have written a concept you have taught. Have them tell something about the concept. Jeopardy, Name that Concept, and Wheel of Fortune are other examples of game formats you can use.

GUIDELINES: Select a student greeter to join you at the door in the mornings for the week. Post the student greeter's name on the front board.

REMINDERS:

- ✓ Remember Funny box or What's Up? box.
- ✓ Remember marble jar.
- ✓ Prepare student interest survey.
- ✓ Continue to call about five parents or guardians each night to say hello, give them the date of the open house, and ask for their support for a great year. Let them know you are available and need their input to be truly effective.

Third Week

Third Week Goals: Reinforce What Is Important

Key Teaching Areas

- ❏ Reinforce management plan.
- ❏ Review correction plan and personal problem/solution plan.
- ❏ Review consequences.
- ❏ Review incentives.
- ❏ Strengthen peer relationships.
- ❏ Develop group cohesiveness.
- ❏ Introduce class meetings.

Success Strategies:

- ❏ Grandma's Rule–First eat your dinner (do your work) and then you can have dessert (reward).
- ❏ Be fair, firm, and friendly.
- ❏ Practice *with-it-ness*.
- ❏ Provide class rewards.
- ❏ When things are going wrong, stop activities and lessons, go back to the management plan, and review or reteach the rules and procedures.

Self-Reflective Opportunities:

- ❏ Maintain an electronic daily or weekly journal. Add reflections at the end of the day or week, which may showcase teaching highlights and stumbling blocks. Make a list of those students needing encouragement.
- ❏ Contact other first-year teachers from your network list and share your experiences with them.

Day 1—Make Guidelines for Giving Directions Work

BEGIN THE DAY: Teacher and student greeter meet the students in the morning.

OPENING ACTIVITIES: Place the reminder cloud or a list on the board to remind students to take attendance, be ready for class, and to begin the routine procedure. Inform the students that we no longer need the reminders for how to begin class. Ask the students for the procedure, step by step if necessary.

ROUTINE PROCEDURE: The morning routine procedure is for the students to get ready for class upon entering the room and to write in their journals.

USE CUE: Raise your hand and move to the front of the room. Continue to monitor the amount of time it takes to get everyone's attention. If students take too much time, take time from students to reinforce this procedure.

GUIDELINES: Review Guidelines for Giving Directions and use this procedure for all directions you give to the students. Especially important are the "give and get" step and the step asking if there are any questions.? Remember, stop the activity if directions were not understood or questions were asked after the steps were finished, and go back to the first step of the procedure and reteach it. Students usually dislike going over items more than once and catch on quickly.

ACTIVITY: Review your teaching style with your students, which is influenced by student input. Discuss survey data and the use of such information. Review the concept of choice. Prepare students to respond to the interest survey with information that will be useful to both students and teacher. Distribute the interest survey. Allow them enough time to complete the survey and have a student from each row collect the surveys. You can use information from the interest survey when greeting students in the mornings and in personalizing the classroom. If the majority of your students like the color yellow, then yellow is what you use for background on your bulletin boards and the color of your posters; and one day a week use yellow paper for the guided practice activities. You can also use the survey information to plan lessons, thematic units, learning centers, projects, and to select library books or feature books for the classroom. The students' responses can help you provide a more appealing classroom learning environment and plan more engaging, interesting, and relevant instruction.

(♣) Interest survey questions to use with special student populations are

- What is your favorite snack?
- What is your favorite color?
- What do you like to do best in school?
- What is your favorite music?
- Where would you like to go on vacation?

(♦) Interest survey questions that are middle school specific are

- What is a recent movie you enjoyed, and what did you like about it?
- What is your favorite music?
- Describe yourself as a friend.

- What is your favorite place to be and why?
- Do you collect anything?

(★) Interest survey questions that can be used for secondary students are

- What do you want to do for a career?
- What would be the title of a book about your life?
- What is the name of someone you admire and why?
- What is something about which you are curious?
- What are your goals for this class?

AFTER-LUNCH IDEAS: Read aloud to students. Begin to alternate this read-aloud time with *sustained silent reading* (SSR) or *drop everything and read* (DEAR) time. Before moving to this SSR or DEAR time, students must have had an opportunity to go to the library or have a well-stocked and relevant in-class library to get books or magazines to read. For younger students, let them get a book or magazine to look at the pictures and predict what the story may be about. Or have them get into pairs and do reciprocal reading or form small groups to read together.

ACTIVITY: Have the students create a hall bulletin board. Students find a picture in a magazine that looks like them or draw a picture or have you take a picture. Place the pictures on a poster, mural, or collage in the hall. Above each picture, the student can make a hat and write his or her name on it. Title the bulletin board "The Fourth Grade Class Is Here "or "The (teacher's name) Bunch Says Hello" or "Hats Off to This Year."

END-OF-THE-DAY ROUTINE: Pass out a rewards survey. The students will take about five minutes and complete the following sentences:

1. Rewards are _____.
2. I think rewards are important because _____.
3. I deserve a reward when _____.
4. Rewards I would like to have are _____.
5. I do not deserve a reward when _____.
6. Another word for reward is _____.

Place the surveys in the students' performance portfolios. For younger students, take one sentence, discuss it with them, and write the words they want to use to complete the sentence. The students read the sentence together or copy it.

REMINDERS:

- ✓ Remember Funny box or What's Up? box.

- ✓ Remember marble jar.

- ✓ Remember colored index cards for *unstuck procedure.*

- ✓ Prepare survey strips—long strips of white paper—with the students' responses to the survey.

- ✓ Prepare name cards of faculty and staff members.

- ✓ Continue to call about five parents or guardians each night to say hello, give them the date of the open house, and ask for their support for a great year.

Day 2—I Believe in Me

BEGIN THE DAY, ROUTINE PROCEDURE, and **USE CUE** are the same each day.

GUIDELINES: Discuss the interest survey information by reporting the class statistics. Get statistics for majority responses. Do a get-acquainted activity. Prepare survey strips by writing each student response on a strip of paper. Allow students to select a strip and try to name the person who made the response. Also include a teacher survey strip. Survey strips can say things such as, "Pizza is my favorite food," "I like to ride my bike," "I play baseball," "I love my video game," or "I take gymnastics."

ACTIVITY: The object of this activity is to introduce the students to other faculty and staff members (principal, librarian, secretary, nurse, janitor, and other teachers). Have students find their buddies. Prepare name cards of faculty and staff and assign each buddy pair to interview one person. In this Think-Pair-Share activity, the pair will work together to develop five interview questions. The teacher needs to edit questions for most learners before the interview is conducted. Students need to make an appointment to interview this person. The appointments should be made sometime during the month of September. Notify the staff and faculty of this project before the students begin making their appointments. The students can share their interview information with the class. The students need to arrange a time with you to share this information.

For younger students, arrange to have staff and faculty people come to the classroom and tell students a little about themselves and their jobs. Encourage the students to ask them questions.

AFTER-LUNCH IDEA: Sustained silent reading (SSR) or drop everything and read (DEAR) time.

Planned Lessons and Activities

Use the established cue to gain everyone's attention. Continue to teach student accountability.

- **Topic**–Problem solving: *5-Step Unstuck Procedure* (Bosch & Kersey, 1993)

- **Opener**–Present students with the following scenario: A student is having a problem with an assignment that a teacher has just given. The assignment needs to be turned in by the end of the class. The student has several choices. What are they?

  List the students' choices on the board. Ask several students what they would choose to do? Why?

- **Objectives**–The student will be able to

  1. List three reasons why problem solvers are needed
  2. Outline the 5-step unstuck procedure
  3. Use the 5-step unstuck procedure

- **Instruction**–Lead a discussion on the importance of problem solving. Why do we need to solve problems? Does it help the student? Does it help the teacher?

  Discuss each step of the 5-step unstuck procedure and ask for examples. The steps are as follows:

  1. Reread the directions.

  2. Go on to the next problem or item. Then go back and complete as much as you can.

  3. Ask the peer assistant for help.

  4. Place a colored index card (signal) on your desk for assistance from the teacher.

  5. Take out a book to read.

Discuss and give everyone a colored index card. The red card means the student needs help from the teacher. Have the students copy the 5-step unstuck procedure and place it in their performance portfolios. Place a poster of the procedure on the front board or wall for the class to use.

- **Guided Practice**–Provide scenarios of student problems. Give some steps taken and omit some steps that should have been taken. Ask students to write down the missing step or steps.

- **Closure**–Give me one reason the 5-step unstuck procedure is important. Give me the first step . . . second step.

- **Independent Practice**–Give older students written scenarios of a student with a problem that can be solved by using the 5-step unstuck procedure. Collect the finished assignments.

(Reprinted with permission of the Helen Dwight Reid Educational Foundation. Published by Heldref Publications, 1319 18th Street, NW, Washington, DC 20036-18020.)

END-OF-THE-DAY ROUTINE: Give the students some sample situations needing correction and ask them, "What is our correction plan?" Situations may be presented for incentives as well. Call out an appropriate or inappropriate behavior and ask for the consequence or incentive to be given. Drop marbles in the jar or add a letter(s) to the secret word if class has learned the management plan.

REMINDERS:

- ✓ Use the Funny box or What's Up? box.

- ✓ Use the marble jar.

- ✓ Begin to document behaviors—attempt to identify the most difficult times or activities.

Day 3—I Will Survive—I Will Succeed

BEGIN THE DAY, ROUTINE PROCEDURE, and **USE CUE** are the same each day.

ACTIVITY: Continue to build positive peer relationships. Have each student draw a name from a hat. Use name cards from the first week. Beneath the name the student writes a positive word (adjective) to describe the student. The name cards are placed on the students' backs. Each student may ask another student three questions that can be answered with a yes or no response. The object is for the students to guess the word written about them.

AFTER-LUNCH IDEAS: Read aloud to students.

Planned Lessons and Activities
Use the established cue to gain everyone's attention.

- **Topic**–Group Cohesiveness

- **Opener**–Show the class pictures of two students and have them look for similarities of the students pictured. Discuss what they have in common, what they share. Ask two students to come to the front of the room and have the class tell how these students are alike. How many have the same color eyes? How many ride the same bus?

For younger students, you will have to find group or class similarities. For example, name things (animals) and have everyone who likes that thing stand up. The class begins to see that they are alike.

- **Objectives**–The student will be able to

  1. Discover similarities among individuals in the class
  2. Examine the similarities of the class as a whole

- **Instruction**–Assign the students to teams (an odd number in each team) and begin working on answering the questions below. The team must answer each question. In other words, they must take the answers of the majority of team members as the team's answer to the question. These team answers will be shared and discussed.

  1. What is the group's favorite color?
  2. What is the group's favorite school subject?
  3. What is the group's favorite sport?
  4. What is the group's favorite television program?
  5. What is the group's special learning interest?

  Continue to examine the similarities of the class as a whole. What similarities are shared by a few teams? What similarities are shared by all the teams?

- **Assessment**–The teacher provides questions using Bloom's verbs and asks students to identify the level (see Bloom's Taxonomy, 1956 or Revised Bloom's Taxonomy, 2001).

- **Closure**–What have we learned from this activity?

  We have many similarities and we share many things. We have this class in common and this teacher. We will be sharing this learning space for the school year. We need to work and learn together.

END-OF-THE-DAY ROUTINE: Say to students, "Tell me what you can do when you get stuck on an assignment?"

REMINDERS:

  ✓ Use marble jar.

  ✓ Begin planning learning centers.

Day 4—Use the Words *We, Our,* and *Us*

BEGIN THE DAY, ROUTINE PROCEDURE, and **USE CUE** are the same each day.

GUIDELINES: The theme for this month is *Freedom*. Discuss how this theme can be developed. The class will develop themes for each month by brainstorming as a whole group activity. Brainstorm one month at a time or for all ten months. Break the class into small groups (four members each) to think of themes. Each group presents ideas and places them on the board. The class will vote on a theme for this month or themes for all ten. The class plans ways to reinforce the themes. For younger students, you'll need to give the themes and have the students plan class activities.

AFTER-LUNCH IDEA: Sustained silent reading (SSR) or drop everything and read (DEAR) time.

Planned Lessons and Activities (✤ ✦ ★ ✳)

Use the established cue to gain everyone's attention. The teacher plans more get-acquainted lessons and activities.

- **Topic**–Getting to Know You

- **Opener**–Present a time line of your life. Ask students to read the events and dates and guess whose time line this is.

- **Objectives**–The student will be able to

  1. Identify items found on a time line
  2. Construct a time line
  3. Create a time line of one's life

- **Instruction**–Present several time lines containing information and show the development of a time line (chronologically). Have students list items found on time lines. As a class, do a time line together from a prepared list of items.

- **Guided Practice**–Have students construct a time line at their seats using a prepared list of items. Monitor the activity. If students can handle the information, proceed to the second objective. If the students are having difficulty, do another example together and have them construct another time line at their seats.

Assessment–Cruise, monitor, and mentor.

Closure–What do time lines tell us about a person? What kinds of things are placed on time lines?

Independent Practice–Tell students, "Write down the key items you want to appear on your time line. Construct a time line of your life and place these items on it." Older students can predict what their time lines might include in the future. When the students are finished, have them put their names at the top of their papers and place the time line on the back bulletin board. Have younger students construct a time line of their life with their parents' or guardians' help.

END-OF-THE-DAY ROUTINE: For closure, model the cues used and ask students what they mean and how students should respond.

REMINDERS:

    ✓ Select computer software to supplement curriculum.

    ✓ Set up learning centers.

    ✓ Prepare *LEAP into Learning Together* poster.

    ✓ Prepare *Class Meeting Agenda* poster.

Day 5—Demonstrate *With-it-ness*

BEGIN THE DAY, ROUTINE PROCEDURE, and **USE CUE** are the same each day.

GUIDELINES: Discuss with the students ways to increase success with cooperative learning. Ask, "How can we be successful in working together and learning together?" Set up a T-graph and list ways to be successful and those that interfere with success. Present LEAP into Learning Together rules for cooperative groups to be successful:

Listen to each other.

Encourage each other to participate.

Accept each group member's ideas.

Praise the thoughts/ideas/work of each member.

Discuss what each letter in LEAP means and how LEAP can work in a group.

(✦ ★ ✤ ✳) Many learners like to do acronym activities as guided practice activities and assignments.

ACTIVITY: Introduce and discuss the reasons for the learning centers. Remind the students that the following procedures are needed as well as the class rules when using the learning centers. Discuss when learning centers are to be used. They can be used if you finish your assigned work, during your free time, and if you come in early or decide to stay late. The learning centers are also assigned weekly as part of a rotation of activities to be completed by the class, groups, and individuals. The learning center procedures are as follows:

1. Four students can work at each learning center. (Determine a maximum number of students that can work at a learning center at a time.)

2. What you begin, you must finish.

3. Put all materials back where they belong when you are finished.

AFTER-LUNCH IDEA: Read aloud to the students.

Planned Lessons and Activities (✤ ✦ ★ ✳)

Use the established cue to gain everyone's attention. Begin to prepare students for the class meeting to be held the third Friday of every month.

- **Topic**–Class Meeting

- **Opener**–Class discussion on students' rights. Say, "What rights in this class are important to you? Rights are important. They are freedoms and they are responsibilities. How can we as a class protect and preserve our rights?

  What are the different forums we can use to protect our rights? Let's plan a democratic process that can serve us. A class meeting is such a process. It provides us with a forum, a designated time, and an amount of time to recognize accomplishments and discuss difficulties, solve problems, and make changes."

- **Objectives**–The student will be able to

  1. Describe a class meeting
  2. Examine the value of class meetings

- **Instruction**–Teach the concept of the class meeting. It is an opportunity to discuss things students like about the class, as well as what might be changed to allow the class to run smoothly. For older students, introduce the agenda for a class meeting.

  A. Class Meeting

     1. Call to order
     2. Minutes taken
     3. Daily items read

  B. Accomplishments recognized

  C. Difficulties reported

  D. Problem solvers

     1. State problem
     2. Brainstorm solutions
     3. Choose a solution
     4. Vote on solution

  E. Adjourn class meeting

The class meeting needs to follow a format. No agenda—no class meeting. If a student has an item to place on the agenda, the item is listed on the poster titled "Class Meeting Agenda." The teacher must put up a new poster each month. Remember to stress that a class meeting is not a gripe session. Tell them, "Each month, on the third Friday, we will have our class meeting. That is the time we will share what works and what is not working in our class. We suggest changes and take it to majority vote. If something important needs to be discussed immediately, we can schedule a special session."

- **Guided Practice**–Have the students copy the agenda and take notes from the discussion. Have students place both items in their performance portfolios where they can refer to them if needed.

- **Assessment**–Cruise and monitor completion.

- **Closure**–Our first class meeting is tomorrow. It will give us an opportunity to see how we can make this activity work.

- **Independent Practice**–Prepare an assignment with true/false statements about freedom and rights. Have the students answer these statements and explain their answers. When students complete the assignment, have them place it in the *In* basket. The assignment will be returned to students tomorrow to discuss, then placed in their performance portfolios.

____1. Freedom is a responsibility.

Explanation _____

____2. Freedom allows me to change things.

Explanation _____

____3. Freedom gives me choices.

Explanation _____

____4. Freedom is for all people.

Explanation _____

____5. Freedom is doing anything I want.

Explanation _____

____6. Freedom is class meetings.

Explanation _____

____7. Freedom is the right to learn without someone interfering with my learning.

Explanation _____

For younger students, take one sentence, discuss it, and write it the way they want to complete it, and read it together or copy it. They can draw a picture or color it.

GUIDELINES: Select a student to be the *computer trainer* to assist other student(s) working on the computer. Allow the student to take software home to preview and become familiar with the program. The computer trainer is to make a class banner (class name) using the computer and display it on the wall.

(♣) **For special student populations, give them extra time to learn how to make a banner using the computer before they become a trainer. Give them a head start on success.**

END-OF-THE-DAY ROUTINE: Say to students, "Tell me one thing you learned today."

REMINDERS:

- ✓ Remember Funny box.
- ✓ Remember the marble jar.
- ✓ Select a new student greeter.
- ✓ Prepare Bloom's Taxonomy chart.

Fourth Week

Fourth Week Goal: Gain Support for What Is Important

Key Teaching Areas

- ❒ Enforce management plan and personal problem solution plan.
- ❒ Strengthen group cohesiveness.
- ❒ Develop class unity and spirit.
- ❒ Build positive peer pressure.
- ❒ Develop class newsletter.

Success Strategies

- ❒ Use cooperative learning.
- ❒ Practice with-it-ness.
- ❒ Review, reteach if necessary, and reinforce consistently the components of your classroom management plan.

Self-Reflective Opportunities:

- ❐ Maintain a daily or weekly journal on the computer and add reflections at the end of the day or week, prior to leaving school, which may showcase teaching highlights and stumbling blocks. Make a list of those students needing encouragement.

- ❐ Place some comments about each lesson at the bottom of your lesson plan book.

- ❐ Contact other first-year teachers from your network list via e-mail or phone and share your experiences with them.

Day 1—Be a Facilitator

BEGIN THE DAY, ROUTINE PROCEDURE, and **USE CUE** are the same each day. Continue to monitor the amount of time it takes to get everyone's attention. If students take too much time, take time from them to reinforce this procedure.

GUIDELINES: Share with students a special class project planned by the teacher: select students each month to read to younger students or classes or students to prepare materials for the school foyer bulletin board. Select two or more students to begin the class project. Allow them to go to the teacher who is participating and set up a time and place to begin this activity. Teachers may want to pair up certain students with students. (✤) **Special population students must be paired in a sensitive manner to ensure that their reading level is above the younger student's level.**

Planned Lessons and Activities

Use the established cue to gain everyone's attention. Introduce Bloom's Taxonomy to the students.

- **Topic**–Bloom's Taxonomy

- **Opener**–Ask students a question that requires a factual answer. Ask them a question that requires an answer of yes or no. Ask them a third question that is an opinion question that can have many answers. Let the students think for a minute about the three questions. Which question was different and why?

- **Objectives**–The student will be able to

  1. Identify the six levels of Bloom's Taxonomy
  2. Develop questions using Bloom's Taxonomy

- **Instruction**–Prepare a poster of Bloom's Taxonomy to be posted in the room for use by the students. The students will be given the levels, sample questions, and verbs to use at the various levels. The students are required to take notes. Ask a few questions and have the students identify the level of the taxonomy. Explain to them that the higher-level questions come from the analysis, synthesis, and evaluation domains. Critical thinking skills are developed through the use of these domains.

- **Guided Practice**–For older students, plan a cooperative learning activity. Go through the Guidelines for Giving Directions and assign students to groups of six. Have each group read a short article and develop questions from the six levels. Assign a level to each student in the group (six students per group and six levels) and ask him or her to be responsible for developing a question based on the article. Together, they put the six questions from the six levels of Bloom's Taxonomy on a sheet of paper to be handed in to the teacher. The members of the group sign their names to the sheet.

- **Closure**–Why is Bloom's Taxonomy important to know and use? Why should questioning come from all levels of the Taxonomy? Who can make up a question from the application domain?

AFTER-LUNCH IDEA: Sustained silent reading (SSR) or drop everything and read (DEAR) time.

ACTIVITY: Explain to the students that the class meeting is scheduled for today. Budget approximately forty-five minutes. The students need to follow the procedures and agenda established. The students will be looking at the management plan. Ask questions such as, "Are the rules effective?" "Are they being followed?" "How are the correction procedures working?" "Do you all feel informed?" "If something is not working, what do we, as a class, do about it?" "When do we present the information?" "How do we go about being heard?"

If the class meeting does not go as planned, stop the meeting and discuss what is happening. Get both student involvement and assistance by asking students what is wrong with the meeting and what is needed to improve the process. Expect appropriate behavior and student accountability. Assist certain students to move toward more self-discipline as well as group accountability. A class norm for behavior and achievement is developed, nurtured, and enforced. Remain consistent in getting students to discuss, correct, and maintain a positive learning environment.

END-OF-THE-DAY ROUTINE: For closure, pass back to the students the freedom and rights assignment. The students can discuss and place the assignment in their performance portfolios.

REMINDERS:

- ✓ Make suggestion/dialogue box.

Day 2—Practice *With-it-ness*

BEGIN THE DAY, ROUTINE PROCEDURE, and **USE CUE** are the same each day.

GUIDELINES: Developing a *suggestion/dialogue box* is another important part of the first few weeks. The suggestion/dialogue box has several purposes. It can be used for suggestions to improve the learning environment and the amount of student learning. It is also a way for the teacher and a student to "talk" confidentially to one another.

A *dialogue time* may be introduced to further the relationship building between students and teacher. Schedule the dialogue time based on need. It can be a whole group activity, a small group activity, or a one-on-one conference time.

AFTER-LUNCH IDEA: Begin reading newspapers—current events—to the class.

ACTIVITY: Prepare students for writing a class newsletter. This activity will reinforce positive peer relationships and group cohesiveness and will develop class unity and spirit by providing a situation for students to work and learn together on a class project. (✤) **For special student populations, be mindful of selecting jobs that are appropriate and will make students feel successful. Such tasks for special education students include illustrating, collating, distributing, and even being the paper-delivery persons.** A newsletter also provides a direct link to the parents and guardians. It is essential to keep the parents and guardians informed and interested in what is going on in the classroom.

Prepare a class newsletter on a monthly (or quarterly) basis to inform the parents and guardians and other interested persons about what is going on in the classroom as reported by the students. Develop the idea of a newsletter by getting student input on topics to be included. Design a name and logo for newsletter. Review several newsletters and decide what to include in the first newsletter. Use a production date of the first of every month.

Have the committees get together to develop the text. The planned lessons each month include the following:

- First meeting—develop text
- Second meeting—share text and agree
- Third meeting—edit material
- Fourth meeting—ready for publication, discuss future copies, additional coverage, and extra features

Use the computer to produce this newsletter. For younger students, the newsletter is a teacher-directed activity. It can be done in a weekly class period or two. Some suggestions for content are the following: names of everyone in the class, unfinished sentences like "I like my class because . . . " or "My favorite animal is . . . ," and writing sentences together about things they have learned. You can put the information into the computer with the students watching you. Give them a chance to type in their names next to the sentences, and so on. Include additional information to alert the parents and guardians to upcoming events. Teachers have commented that the newsletter always makes it home, whereas teacher-written notices or handouts seldom reach their proper destination.

END-OF-THE-DAY ROUTINE: For closure, ask students, "What is class spirit? What are our class projects? What do you like best about this class?"

REMINDERS:

- ✓ Remember Funny box or What's Up? box.
- ✓ Remember marble jar.
- ✓ Begin peer tutoring.
- ✓ Prepare application forms for peer tutors.

Day 3—Be Proactive, Not Reactive

BEGIN THE DAY, ROUTINE PROCEDURE, and **USE CUE** are the same each day.

AFTER-LUNCH IDEAS: Distribute newspapers and have the students silently read an article. Discuss if they liked the article and whether it was easy to read. Depending on your grade level, you may have to provide information about what to read the first time and move them along carefully in choosing what they want to read. You don't want students to choose items too difficult to read and understand. Prepare students for the upcoming after-lunch ideas on Friday, in which they will read a short article from a newspaper or magazine and tell the class why they read it.

Planned Lessons and Activities (✤ ✦ ★ ✱)

Use the established cue to gain everyone's attention.

- **Topic**–Prepare Students for Writing a Newsletter
- **Opener**–Discuss with students the idea of a class newsletter. Put the word *newsletter* in a word cloud and brainstorm areas that could be covered in the newsletter.
- **Objectives**–The student will be able to
    1. Identify areas for the newsletter
    2. Develop job tasks for committees

- **Instruction**–Areas that need to be covered include math, language arts, science, social studies, and other areas of interest; announcements; future projects; and activities. You must remind the students that the newsletter should contain high-quality writing and each of them should take on the role of reporter. Everyone is to be involved and all names are to be included in every issue. Have them take notes, and begin to think of what to include under each area. Move toward developing committees, each with a specific focus (e.g., committee for science, committee for special interests) and certain tasks that must be completed. Ask the students to choose a reporter on the six o'clock news to follow as they look at the role of reporting. (Assign students to committees on the basis of the interest surveys and their participation in the get-acquainted activities.)

- **Assessment**–Scan, cruise, monitor, and mentor, and question and answer.

- **Closure**–Tell me the areas chosen for the newsletter. What are some of the tasks developed for the committees?

END-OF-THE-DAY ROUTINE: Ask the students, "How does the management plan (rules, correction, incentives) give you freedom?"

REMINDERS:

- ✓ Remember marble jar.

- ✓ Select peer tutors for the month.

- ✓ Select tutors from applications.

- ✓ Plan peer tutor training.

Day 4—Be Pleased

BEGIN THE DAY, ROUTINE PROCEDURE, and **USE CUE** are the same each day.

AFTER-LUNCH IDEAS: Read aloud a newspaper article. After reading, tell the students why you liked the article. This should prepare them for Friday when they are to read newspaper articles and tell the class why they liked them. Set up a scheduled reading time for students. Plan help sessions for students to read with you and to go over information prior to their reading time. (♣ ♦ ★ ✳) A sample worksheet is provided that can be used for all learners (see Figure 5.12).

ACTIVITY: Continue to prepare students for writing the newsletter. Prepare a poster with each committee and the tasks to be completed in groups. Review the guidelines for giving directions and LEAP rules, and direct the students through the procedure. Assign members to committees to develop a rough draft. Each group places a rough

FIGURE 5.12   *5 Ws Worksheet*

Name: _____

Date: _____

Please write a sentence for each *W* word below.

Name of your article _____

WHO: _____

_____

_____

WHAT: _____

_____

_____

WHEN: _____

_____

_____

WHERE: _____

_____

_____

WHY: _____

_____

_____

OPINION: _____

_____

_____

draft in the file under the bulletin board titled "Our Class Newsletter." Circulate a piece of colored paper listing the committees and have the members sign their names under their committee. Place the committee sign-up sheet on the bulletin board. Newsletters, as they are completed, will be placed on this bulletin board as well.

END-OF-THE-DAY ROUTINE: Say to students, "Tell me something you would like to learn more about. Tell me something you learned today in math and English."

REMINDERS:

✓ Remember Funny box or What's Up? box.

✓ Remember marble jar.

Day 5—I Believe the Children Are Our Future

BEGIN THE DAY, ROUTINE PROCEDURE, and **USE CUE** are the same each day.

GUIDELINES: Discuss the role of a *peer tutor*. Show students the application form for the position. Discuss the job description, qualities needed, and requirements. Give students a deadline for returning applications. Add this information to October's monthly planning, day 1, under the Guidelines section. Once you've received the applications, select the first group of peer tutors. Plan an after-school training session for the peer tutors. Each peer tutor will select and train an assistant tutor. The assistant tutor will assume tutoring responsibilities the following month. Then that peer tutor selects an assistant and the process continues.

ACTIVITY: Review the guidelines for giving directions and have the committees once again edit the rough draft of the newsletter. Have the students share the articles with the class and get final approval of the newsletter.

AFTER-LUNCH IDEA: SSR time reading newspapers and magazine articles.

GUIDELINES: Discuss special days with the class and have them plan a "yellow day" (students wear yellow and work on yellow paper), "sports day" (wear something related to sports), and "twin day" (wear matching clothes and work in pairs).

END-OF-THE-DAY ROUTINE: For closure, ask the students, "If someone new came to our class, what information can you share with him or her about our class? Which class member is responsible for new students?"

REMINDERS:

✓ Remember to use Funny box.

✓ Remember to use marble jar.

✓ Assign student greeter.

Continue the management plan into the second month. See that the format continues and new ideas are inserted. Additional ideas are presented for possible inclusion into the management plan at a later date.

End of the First Month

This ends the first month of your first year of teaching. It is time to plan for the next thirty days, and the next, and the next. Use this same outline and plug in new management material. At the beginning of each month, you need to review the last month's information, ideas, and activities. Continue to make a list of the reminders after each day for the next day. Below are partial lists of reminders and new ideas to start you into the next month.

REMINDERS:

✓ Prepare assignment sheet or calendar.

✓ Use peer tutors and assign a peer tutor for November.

✓ Use computer tutors and assign a computer tutor for November.

✓ Use the established cue to gain everyone's attention for teaching a lesson.

✓ Remember the class meeting on the third Friday of the month.

✓ Remember Funny box and marble jar.

✓ Remember class projects: reading to students, bulletin board, and the class newsletter.

✓ Remember newsletter development during a month:

  • First meeting—develop text

  • Second meeting—share text and agree

  • Third meeting—edit material

  • Fourth meeting—ready for publication and discuss future copies, additional coverage, and extra features

✓ Plan to have past tutors train new tutors one day after school.

New Ideas

Here are more ideas for possible inclusion in the management plan in the months to follow:

• Schedule *Teacher Help* sessions.

• Hold a *Student Teaching Day*—The students will be given the opportunity to teach the class a lesson. They will be given the topic to teach and have fifteen minutes to teach it. The topic will support your planned lessons. (✤) **This is an excellent activity for special student populations as well, but plan for more teacher assistance.**

- Teach the Lesson Plan Outline (see Figure 5.1). Share the outline with the students and discuss what it means to the teacher and to the students. Highlight roles of the teacher and the student in learning. It is important to demonstrate accountability in the teaching and learning processes as well as to establish a sense of ownership, responsibility, control, and power for one's own learning. The format includes the following: topic, opener, objectives, instruction, guided practice, assessment, closure, and independent practice.

- Refrain from using mega search tools such as Google to locate lesson plans on the Internet. Rather, use these well-respected and juried sites for wonderful resources for your classroom. Visit the following sites:

Discovery Channel: https://www.discoveryeducation.com/teachers/free-lesson-plans

DMA Foldables: http://www.dinah.com

edHelper: http://www.edhelper.com

Education World: http://www.educationworld.com

Kathy Schrock's Guide: http://www.schrockguide.net

Lesson Plans: http://lessonplanspage.com

PBS Teachers: http://www.pbslearningmedia.org

Scholastic Lesson Plans: http://www.scholastic.com/teachers/lesson-plans/free-lesson-plans

Share My Lesson: http://www.sharemylesson.com

Teachers.Net: http://teachers.net/lessons

You will be adding more management ideas to the plan that will continually improve how the class works. The management ideas need to be taught and practiced. Intersperse those planned lessons with the curriculum lessons.

Being a good classroom manager throughout the year will increase student efficiency and productivity.

III. Comments From First-Year Teachers

The 30-day management plan was field tested by twenty-five first-year teachers, and their feedback has been incorporated into the plan. Some of these comments are shared below. The comments can serve as a confidence booster and, possibly, as an incentive for you to continue with the plan in the following months.

Kim (5th Grade): My first week has been absolutely fantastic. I taught the rules the first week and my cue. My cue is to raise my hand. They look at me, raise their hand, and close their mouths. It works in the room, in line, in the hallway, and even in the gym. The most amazing thing to me is that they try to quiet each other down and when I'm walking to the front of the room, they are already raising their hands.

Joan (6th Grade): My students loved the class puzzle activity. I used puzzle glue and displayed the puzzle in the classroom. When we are not working together, I refer to the puzzle and we discuss it.

Morgan (secondary, special education): I always use a cue to begin instruction. The cue I have chosen is to walk to the front of the room and hold up the book or homework folder of the first or next subject. I time the response with a stopwatch and place the amount of time taken on the chalkboard. No reward is attached; students just like to get a "good" time or "beat" their last time.

Imelda (5th Grade): I have realized that there are not enough corners in the room to send the disruptive students, so correction isn't enough. That is why a management plan is so essential.

Kelly (secondary): This management plan works! We practiced and I reviewed and retaught the plan when necessary. The veteran teachers in my building were telling me that I didn't look or act like a first-year teacher. They were saying things like, "You are in control," and "You follow through." Words like these are great for a first-year teacher's ego and to carry you through your bad days. Many teachers in my building wanted to see this management plan and get a copy of it. My principal mentioned that he would like all of his teachers in his school using this plan.

Cynthia (5th Grade): The plan gave me the confidence I needed. I knew what to do. I looked good!

Lisa (8th Grade): My team member and I were called the "Mighty Mites" by our principal. We both are short in stature, but we were very much in control. We followed the management plan and felt we were together in philosophy, expectations, and operation. The consistency was empowering.

Diane (elementary): This is my second year of teaching. The first year, I did not have a management plan and I took the "Wimp" approach. I did what the other teachers told me to do for rules and discipline as I certainly did not want to alienate them. I was not happy and extremely inconsistent. This year, with the plan, I have a guide and directions for putting together my real first year of teaching—my way!

Jennifer (Kindergarten): I was worried about knowing what and how to do what is needed. You get the books and materials for the academic part of teaching, but you can't teach without managing. The management plan helped me pull it all together. I like my start.

The pilot group admitted they felt the pressure as first-year teachers to teach less management and push academics immediately. They expressed concern about keeping up with the rest of the teachers and being on the same pages, if not ahead of them, in the books. To accommodate this need and concern, spread the introduction of the management over a longer period of time than the thirty days. Don't stop because of the pressure to move through the curriculum at the same pace as your counterparts. The first-year teacher must realize the first one or two chapters of the textbooks are designed to be review. This should afford you the time to concentrate on management. When feeling the pressure to be on the same pages in the books as your colleagues, plan to gain pages by truly reviewing and not requiring that students complete every page, problem, activity, and exercise. Teaching your management plan will result in a true readiness for teaching academics.

The overall responses to the classroom management plan were positive. The first-year teachers involved in the field-based study agreed that they felt prepared to teach the curriculum with a management emphasis. Interestingly, most of the teachers felt that they were taught how to write lesson plans but never heard of writing management lesson plans. Many first-year teachers cited that the schools gave them textbooks, manuals, and curriculum guides to direct their efforts in teaching but nothing to help them with teaching classroom management. They all agreed that the management plan gave them the needed direction and confidence in managing student behavior, student learning, and the day-to-day operation of the classroom. The first-year teachers reported that they now know how to take control, be in control, and plan for such control. *The First-Year Teacher* and the 30-day classroom management plan provide assistance, affirmation, and assurance that a teacher can have a good beginning to the first year.

Beginning teachers suffer alone through numerous problems and operate under a considerable amount of stress, anxiety, and unrealistic self-imposed expectations. Many first-year teachers cope with the most difficult students, take on time-consuming extracurricular activities, and are named to several school committees. Every teacher must teach in a manner that *fits* his or her own personality. Beginning teachers must develop a plan and be prepared before entering the classroom door.

CHAPTER SIX

How Can I Do It All?

I. Time Management

One of the advantages that seasoned teachers have is their ability to learn from their experiences. Most teachers have figured out what is important and what can be ignored. Most teachers have developed many shortcuts for the administrative and instructional classroom tasks. This chapter is one that is to be read after the first semester of your first year. Many new teachers have shared that they are not ready for shortcuts when they start their first year of teaching. One new teacher commented that she didn't know how anyone could think about saving time in the beginning, when you are not sure of what to do or how to do it. Over your winter break, relax with this chapter. During this break time, you are now ready to think about developing your own shortcuts or reading some articles on time-savers for teachers. You will know which ideas will work for you. Many time-saving ideas can find their way into your classroom in January.

The purpose of this chapter is to give you, the first-year teacher, the benefit of reading many of the tricks of the trade from seasoned teachers. In every instance, these classroom veterans indicated that they wished other teachers had shared with them some of the ways to make teaching more enjoyable and their work more manageable very early in their careers.

The authors have conducted many workshops for teachers. At break time in one of those workshops, a young, male teacher who had just completed his first year of teaching six classes of history at the secondary level asked us for some advice. He admitted he was overwhelmed and that his first year was not successful. Because the class was composed of mostly experienced teachers, we prompted an "Ann Landers" advice session. It was difficult for this teacher to ask for help or advice because he was afraid others would see him as a failure. To his surprise, when he began to share some experiences from his first year of teaching, the experienced teachers were very sympathetic and provided a wealth of information for him to use in his second year.

For example, one concern he shared was that he was deluged with administrative paperwork and student papers, reports, and projects to grade. He would go home with stacks—150 or more papers—to correct. One teacher asked if he made due dates the same for each class. He quickly said that he did. She commented that different due dates would allow him to correct fewer papers at one time. It was like a light bulb had been turned on. It seemed like such a simple solution, but it was one that had not occurred to him.

Often, first-year teachers fail to see ways to make things easier for themselves. Many new teachers are not comfortable asking for help or advice from other teachers. The veteran teachers whom I have surveyed have been quite willing to share time-management strategies they have found to be useful—ways of cutting down or cutting out wasted time and energy. Practicing teachers know that using these ideas called *tricks of the trade*, *shortcuts*, or *time-savers* can create time for more important teaching efforts. Time-saving ideas can reduce some of the paperwork demands and add a level of efficiency to the daily tasks of managing a classroom.

Technology must be an active partner in your plans for incorporating time-saving ideas into your classroom. Use technology to produce labels for any of the organizer tips you read in this text. The labels can be colorful, with appropriate graphics, and can be reprinted if they ever become tired or look worn out. Use a graphic organizer program to map the flow of a typical day in your classroom, or the actual classroom layout indicating areas of specific activities and storage locations for materials and supplies. Print out copies of your class rosters with checkboxes for attendance and lunch count. Have students check off these boxes as part of their morning routine.

If you have a classroom library, keep a file of all your titles using Excel or some other spreadsheet program. In the actual library area, include a checkout list for students with columns for their name, book title, and out and in dates. Teach them to use this system and have a classroom helper check the list at the end of each day. Once a month, tally the number of times a book has been checked out and use this information to order additional copies if necessary or to have a "book chat."

The contents in this chapter should save you some time. Read the ideas and highlight the ones that appeal to you. The second semester, or January, is fast approaching and you want to make some positive changes in the way your class works.

II. Time-Saver Ideas From Teachers

The following are the time-saver ideas that many veteran teachers have learned over the years and want to share with you. Some ideas can be implemented immediately; others may be useful later in the second semester or the following year.

Organizing Ideas

- Provide each child with a pocket folder to take work back and forth from home. Use one side of the folder for school work and the other for newsletters, calendars, and messages. These folders can be laminated and slit at the pockets for more durability.

- Make student flip files for organizing and sorting student work and information. The materials needed for the files are ½ of a file folder (the side with tab), a long strip of poster board (about one inch wider than the folders—12 ½" x 18"), and clear tape. Position folders about one inch apart on a poster board strip. Tape the edge of the folder half to the strip, taping on front and back. Place the student's name on the folder tab. Fifteen flip files on one strip of poster board would be the maximum one can hold.

- Purchase a crate and put in hanging folders labeled with each student's name. In the folder are manila files labeled with subjects. When any work is done, it is put in the folders. All work and tests are numbered. Then, when it is time to study for a test, tell the students to study 1 through 5 or 6, 7, and 10.

- Provide a routine for children when they come into the classroom. Ask the children to sharpen pencils when they arrive at school in the morning before the bell rings. (They usually have ten to fifteen minutes between bus arrival and the morning bell.) When the pencil sharpener is not to be used (after the bell), cover it with a sock. The children then know not to approach the sharpener and not to ask.

- Use *in* and *out* pencil cans. Students may place a pencil that has a broken point or needs sharpening into the in can and take a newly sharpened pencil from the out can to use. This saves time, assures the student of always having a sharpened pencil, and provides an opportunity for a student-helper to sharpen all the pencils at a designated time.

- Purchase some clothespins. In the classroom, each student has a clothespin with his or her name on it. Have a bulletin board with library pockets denoting different destinations, such as chorus, patrols, newspaper committees, bathroom, band, and so on. When students leave the room, they clip their clothespin to the appropriate pocket. This works well for some teachers and cuts down on having to rely on memory.

- This may seem time consuming, but in reality it saves time. Put all class units in binders. Organize the units by day and include lesson plans and worksheets needed for each lesson. It is a real time-saver to not have to look for all the pieces when the time to teach the lesson comes.

- A successful, time-saving technique in the classroom is to assign each student a number determined by the alphabetical order in which his or her name is listed in the class roster. When a new student arrives, the next number after the others on the class roster is assigned. Each time a student does an assignment, whether it is class work or a test, the student writes the number in the top right-hand corner of the paper. This system serves the following five purposes:

1. The students can take turns filing papers in numerical order.

2. The children line up according to their numbers. Call numbers by groups, for example, "One through five may line up."

3. Use the Popsicle sticks to choose students to be special helpers, messengers, and game participants, and to select students for answering questions and building teams. It is a fair method to use because students are selected strictly by chance and it eliminates the likelihood of someone becoming a teacher's pet. The "used" sticks remain out of the can until all have been chosen.

4. When collecting assignments, they are easily put in order, and if a number is missing, the teacher can tell immediately who has not turned in the work.

5. Sometimes use individual mailboxes for paper distribution. The children know that the numbers also correspond with the mailboxes and are able to help file both quickly and efficiently in their spare time.

There seem to be endless possibilities for this lottery-type number system, from choosing a line leader to choosing the student to say the Pledge of Allegiance at the open house or give morning announcements on the PA system with the principal.

Attendance Ideas

- Use clothespins to quickly check attendance and lunch count. Each child has a clothespin with his or her name on it. These are clipped on the *Absence Chart* (see Figure 6.1) prior to the beginning of each day. This chart is placed by the door so that the students can move their clothespin to the "I'm buying lunch" section or the "I'm here today" section. You only need to glance at the chart to get attendance and the lunch count.

FIGURE 6.1 *Absence Chart*

I'm absent	I'm buying lunch	I'm here today

- Plan taking attendance with a simple system (see Figure 6.2). Instead of checking each person as present or absent in the attendance book each day, only fill in the date when the person is absent. If the student comes in late, circle the date to indicate that the student was only tardy. This makes it very easy to fill in the absentee/tardy section on report cards and student records and saves a lot of time.

- When two groups of students come to the classroom and two children share the same desk, laminate name tags with the name of the child from the morning class on one side and the name of the child from the afternoon class on the other. Put a piece of Velcro on the corner of the desk and a piece on each side of the name tag. The children put their names on the desks when they enter the room. They place the name tag in the desk when they leave the room. You can see the names on the desks better and can take roll faster. Older students prefer name tags on their desks rather than on their clothing.

- Make bus posters. Laminate several large yellow buses for the room and then place a number on the side of each bus. Cut out people and write on them the names of the students who are riding that bus. Above the buses, write "Bus Business."

  While standing in line waiting for the buses, students sing and draw shapes in the air, sing vowel jingles, and count by fives and tens.

Room Readiness Ideas

- Whenever deciding to move students to another place in the room, instead of rearranging desks, reassign them. This forces students to clear out their desks and make a clean start in another location.

FIGURE 6.2 *Attendance Book System*

John	5/17	6/2	(6/5)					
Susie								
Jack	4/19	6/2	6/3	6/4	6/5			

- When the class needs a quick cleanup, play a game! Choose two students (volunteers or draw Popsicle sticks) to stand back-to-back until the teacher says, "GO." Give the pair thirty seconds to pick up paper scraps, pencils, or crayons. After the thirty seconds have elapsed, the students compare who has the most items. The winner gets a sticker (or other treat). If there is still a need for additional cleanup, select two more students. Rule: Running causes immediate disqualification.

- Keep a small spray bottle of fingernail polish remover to use for wiping off lines from permanent markers from any laminated surface.

- Use tennis balls as bumpers on the legs of the chairs to keep the noise down and add color and fun to the room. They are slit and placed on the chair legs. Old tennis balls can be provided by the students or parents and guardians.

Classroom Management Ideas

- Begin each school day with journal time. As the children enter, after unpacking, they are expected to write in their journals. Soft music makes this a relaxed and enjoyable time. This starts the day quietly and reflectively and gives the students an opportunity to express some unresolved feelings they may have experienced at home or on the way to school. This can be followed with a sharing time.

- After the first few weeks of school, when classroom routine has settled down to a predictable pattern, create a master form for each day of the week and run off several copies. Since many regular events occur once a week on the same day, fill in the set schedule and basic information or instructions and leave space for the specifics for that day. This helps in writing up lessons plans quickly and is invaluable to a substitute if you have to miss school unexpectedly.

- One of the projects used in a sixth-grade classroom to help students gain a sense of responsibility is to set aside time for them to work with kindergarten students. Some of the activities include writing stories the kindergarten students dictate, reading to the students, and playing educational games dealing with numbers and letters.

- Ask to have an older student from another class read to your class. A first-grade teacher, whose students were very rowdy every day after lunch, asked the teacher of a third-grade class if one student could come each day to her classroom to read to the children when they returned from lunch. The third-graders took the book home (The teachers chose the **Boxcar Children** series, by Gertrude Chandler Warner, to read) and practiced reading at night to be prepared. The first-graders started returning eagerly from lunch. They put their lunch boxes away quickly and sat down on the rug to listen to the reader of the day. The third-grade teacher reported that oral reading skills improved and even the most timid students in the classroom began to ask for a turn to read. The younger students made bookmarks for the third-grade classroom and gave them awards for being "Reading Friends."

- When the whole class is interacting or talking, raise your hand. When the children see your hand, they raise their hands and get quiet. This spreads around the classroom very quickly. The best part is not having to say a word or lose patience. When your hand goes down, the class should remain silent until further directions. This should be presented as a game. It's important to use this in a positive manner, praising the students who raise their hands first.

- One attention-getting device to use if the children are not following directions is to whisper something positive in the ear of one or two who are listening. For example, just walk over and whisper, "Sally, I like the way you are standing quietly waiting for the next set of instructions," or whisper, "Thanks, Billy, for holding on to the ball and not bouncing it." The other children stop what they are doing because they want to hear what was whispered to the others.

- One teacher is known as the "sticker lady" in her classroom, always having her pockets filled with stickers. Many times when she sees children who are obeying the rules, she places a sticker on a notecard taped to the student's desk and verbalizes what she likes about what they are doing. This makes the other children take notice and mimic the rewarded behavior. This is especially helpful when establishing new behaviors.

- Clap a rhythm to get the children's attention. They clap the rhythm back. Continue this until all are quiet and paying attention. Changing the rhythm makes it more interesting.

- One effective behavioral management technique is earning marbles. This method involves positive reinforcement of the whole class. When everyone is following the class rules, they will be rewarded by having a marble transferred from one jar to another. This behavioral technique has several successive steps. The first step is to earn ten marbles. Have two jars on your desk in front of the room. One jar is empty. The other jar is filled with marbles. When the whole class is following the rules, reward them by taking a marble out of the full jar and dropping it into the empty jar.

Reward their good behavior often and they quickly earn the ten marbles. When the tenth marble has been earned, stop whatever it is the class is doing and either go outside or stay inside and have free time. A marble earned cannot be taken away. After the students have earned the ten marbles, they are put back into the first jar and start again. This time they must earn thirty marbles. When they do, stop and have free time. The third step is to have all the marbles from one jar transferred to the other jar. When the last marble has been dropped into the jar, stop what the class is doing and choose a "big treat"—a snack and a movie, drawing, reading, or playing games.

- Sometimes you may find it necessary to offer visual reminders of behavior agreements. Behavior contracts (see Figures 6.3 and 6.4) work well because they remind students that their behavior is their choice.

- Each month, reserve half of a bulletin board for a candy calendar. Attach seasonal candies to the calendar, one for each school day of the week. Small stickers, which represent free homework passes, are hidden behind six of the candies. At the end of the day, a drawing is held to see who wins the candy. To be eligible for the drawing, students must have displayed good behavior during the day, completed all assignments, and obeyed class rules. (They can keep their own points during the day—and the teacher announces how many points they must have to be eligible for the drawing.) A different person draws each day, but only when everyone is seated and ready to go home. The candy calendar really makes for a quick, quiet dismissal. Students will never let you forget it!

- In my classroom, I use a class meeting technique. If there is a problem with one child hurting another or fighting in the class, a student can call all together in problem-solving a way to handle the situation. When everyone is together (on the rug or other designated place), ask the child who called the meeting to explain the problem as he or she saw it. After all sides have had a chance to explain or defend themselves, the children help you decide whether or not there should be consequences. The children are usually very fair and listen to their peers. The consequences range from missing ten minutes of free time to writing an apology note to the hurt friend.

- In a high school class, require a student to take daily notes of the class instruction. This is similar to taking the minutes at meetings. Give everyone an opportunity to be the notetaker and as an incentive, they earn points toward their semester grade. Some students, of course, want to do it more often for the incentive. Once everyone has done it, take volunteers. The notes are written neatly and in an organized fashion and kept in a class notebook, which gives everyone an opportunity to read or copy the notes. This is especially helpful for students who are absent and want to know what they have missed. Students and parents or guardians can refer to the book to review instruction, recall assignments, check homework assignments, or remember due dates.

- If children are having a hard time focusing on reading (in a reading group), the teacher might go to the dollar store and buy a bunch of sunglasses. She can pop the lenses out of the glasses, and let the children wear the frames when they are in a reading group. This often helps the children to focus, and they feel very special when they are given the glasses to wear.

FIGURE 6.3   *Sample Behavior Contract*

I will remember not to forget my contract

For: _____

I will be in my seat when the bell rings—for five consecutive days.

_____ (student) will help to remind me.

My teacher will help by saying "I like the way _____ is in (his or her) seat before the bell rings."

To celebrate, I will be able to be line leader for five consecutive days.

Date: _____

Helper: _____

Teacher: _____

FIGURE 6.4   *Sample Behavior Contract*

Work Contract

I'm jumping to say . . .

When: I can recite the multiplication tables for 6 and 7.

Then: I can get a homework pass.

Date: _____

My name: _____

Teacher's name: _____

Contract reviewed on (date): _____

- Buy enough whiteboards and dry erase markers for each child to have one. When you are reviewing a lesson (math, spelling, science, social studies, etc.), ask each child to write the answer on the board. Then the children can hold their boards up in the air and you can look around the room quickly to see which children have the right answer. You can let them keep their own scores and grant certain privileges to the children who get the most right—or the team that has the most points. Children can erase their boards with old socks that they keep in their desks. The benefits of these boards are many. Children love to write on whiteboards. The teacher can quickly see which children know the answers and which need extra help. The chance that all the children will stay focused is much higher—since you are asking for answers from all of them—as opposed to asking one child to answer a question (and running the risk of losing the other children's interest). Many classrooms now have smart boards (interactive white boards) that allow students to come to the board and with smart board pens make notations on the board.

Parent or Guardian Communication

- Use many student interest surveys, for example, when conferencing with students or speaking with parents or guardians. Also include them in the student portfolios. The information you received from the surveys is very useful for planning units and activities and for goal setting. You can personalize the curriculum to the needs and interests of the students.

- Send home a Teacher's Report Card (see Figure 6.5), which helps you in planning for the following year and lets the parents or guardians know you are concerned about your performance and self-improvement. This form can be modified and completed by students as well.

- Use the website **www.teacherease.com** as a grade book. Parents or guardians can log in at any time to see their child's grades and can e-mail you at school directly. Also send announcements that way. There are reports that you can run and it will average scores. It does cost money.

- Send weekly reports home to let the parents or guardians see their child's progress. This is not too much of a hassle if you find or design a simple form to use. (See Figure 6.6 for a sample of a reading log.)

Our readers have provided some ideas that are fun, take little time to organize, require few if any supplies, and meet with almost everyone's approval.

- A fun game you can play with almost any subject is baseball. Divide the class into two teams. Put one team up to bat while the other sits quietly in their seats and listens. You are the pitcher, and one by one the team that is up to bat comes to home plate for the question. It can be "What is 5 times 5?" "What is the capital of Virginia?" "How do you spell *mechanical*?" or "What are the three parts of an insect?" If the batter gets the answer right, he moves to first base. If the batter misses the question, that is one "out." Teams can make runs and keep score—on the board—for the day or the week. One **very important** rule

FIGURE 6.5   *Teacher's Report Card*

A+

Dear Parents or Guardians,

Please take a few minutes to complete this report card. Thank you for your assessment.

Grading Scale

A = Excellent   B = Good

C = Average   NI = Needs Improvement

- Did your child learn a lot of valuable information?

    A _____
    B _____
    C _____
    NI _____

- Did your child get more interested in his or her learning?

    A _____
    B _____
    C _____
    NI _____

- Did your child enjoy school more this year?

    A _____
    B _____
    C _____
    NI _____

- How do you feel about the amount of homework assigned?

    A _____
    B _____
    C _____
    NI _____

- Indicate an overall teaching grade.

    A _____
    B _____
    C _____
    NI _____

Comments:

Signature: _____

FIGURE 6.6   *Sample Reading Log*

My Reading Log

Books Completed	Started	Finished	Comments

is that if there is any yelling, arguing, commotion, talking out, or coaching, for instance, that is one out for that team—even if that team is the one in the field (at their desks). (You will **have** to enforce this rule if the game is to work effectively.) Since the teacher is the pitcher, you will have some control over which children get the harder questions.

- Play Who Wants To Be A Millionaire? Divide the class into two groups. First, ask all children to order certain events, such as the Vietnam War, the Civil War, World War I, and World War II. See how many children on each team get the correct answer. Then the team with the most points can select one person to be the first contestant. That contestant can use three life lines if help is needed: (1) choose from one of five people, (2) ask his whole team, or (3) ask for 50/50 (where two of the answers are erased, leaving only two choices). Of course, the questions are the review in any subject of your choice—social studies, geography, history, or math. The million dollar prize could be a $100,000 candy bar. When the contestant misses a question, the other team puts up their contestant and the same rules apply.

- The games Concentration, Jeopardy, and Bingo can also be adapted for review sessions. You can design them so that children can play them alone, in pairs, or in groups.

III. More Time-Saver Tips

Time management is critical to a teacher's efficiency and productivity. Parks (1998, p. 46) refers to time-savers as "sanity savers." He provides seven steps to taking control of your time:

1. Identify time robbers.

2. Learn to say no.

3. Enlist students to help.

4. Schedule recoup time into your planning book.

5. Turn elephants into hors d'oeuvres (cut huge tasks into smaller ones).

6. Fight procrastination with the 7/11 technique (subdivide tasks into priority A or B with A being smaller tasks, and B being the larger tasks. Next, spend seven minutes on an A task and then switch for eleven minutes to a B task).

7. Don't feel guilty.

Plan a trip to a library or search online for teacher educational journals. Find the August, September, and January issues to look for articles on time-savers. An article titled, "Six Quick Tips for Success," by Gruber and Gruber (2002, pp. 80–81) is especially helpful in areas of paper and time management. The authors remind teachers that there will always be more work to do, and finding ways to save time will allow you to have a life beyond teaching. In an issue of **Education Digest** (Time Savers, 1995), Virginia educators and a few teachers from outside the state provided a long list of time-savers for educators. The tips are practical and worth your time to read. Highlight the ones you can use in your classroom. Hennick (1999, pp. 36–40) in his article, "11 Magic Tricks for New Teachers," provides the following time-saving suggestions (You'll also find summarized specifics after each magic trick):

1. **Beg, borrow, and steal**—It isn't necessary to reinvent the wheel. Learning from each other is part of good teaching.

2. **Spend time to save time**—Take the time as the school year starts to put classroom management in place.

3. **Get organized**—Set up file folders, labeled or color-coded, to reduce and/or organize the clutter.

4. **Prevent behavior issues**—Planning, teaching, and enforcing a classroom management plan—rules, routines, procedures, consequences, and incentives—are important for consistency. Bosch (2006) reminds teachers that a management plan is needed to prevent student misbehavior.

5. **Use your minutes**—Time used in school is less time spent on school work at home.

6. **Delegate**—Your students can become the best of helpers.

7. **Learn to say no**—Practice saying that you can't take on any more responsibilities because this is your first year of teaching.

8. **Avoid perfection**—Keep to the task and remember KISS—Keep It Short and Simple!

9. **Streamline parent or guardian communication**—Copy some simple forms to use or have forms with fill-in blanks that are ready at all times and for all things.

10. **Grade smarter**—Grade certain papers and allow others to remain ungraded. For practice, use rubrics and self-grading forms when appropriate.

11. **Get a life**—You need to use time-savers, as they are critical to getting the job done in a timely way. There is life outside of the classroom.

According to Burrall (2006, p. 11), technology can save teachers valuable time, beginning with simply using e-mail. He continues to estimate a time saving of three to four hours per week if you use a digital calendar, one to two hours if you program a voicemail message, and one hour per week if you use many desktop applications.

Using the computer can save time, and many classroom tasks can be done by paraeducators, parents and guardians, and students.

Teachers need ideas called time-savers, sanity savers, or lifesavers to make the class work more efficiently and effectively. Teachers also need to support each other by sharing ideas on what works in the classroom. We read words in our textbooks and manuals; we acquire actions from other teachers.

CHAPTER SEVEN

How Do I End the Year?

I. Count Down: The Last Month

Pauly (2002, p. 284), an eighth-grade teacher, laments over why no one warned her about what it is like at the end of the school year. She writes,

> *The lovely eighth-graders I had as students up until spring break had disappeared. They were replaced by bundles of hormones eagerly anticipating the coming of summer and high school. They were far too grown up at this point for any lame 'middle school' unit I had planned for them. I had read somewhere that eighth-grade students attempt to cut their ties to middle school toward the end of the year by being particularly unpleasant to be around—supposedly to make their transition to high school easier. I thought this sounded like a reasonable explanation for such change[d] behaviors and attitudes, so I gave the students a little extra space. I figured I could use some extra room myself, because recently I hadn't been particularly pleasant to be around either. Meanwhile, I was hoping the top of my desk still existed somewhere beneath the stack of end-of-the-year reports consuming it.*

It seems that the end of the year requires as much planning as the beginning of the year. Everyone is tired. Time is running out. The paperwork demands are extreme. The students are ready to go, but they have to stay a few more days. It has been said that the months of May and June are as challenging for experienced teachers as they are for first-year teachers. In talking with many veteran teachers, they suggest teachers plan to invite resource or guest speakers to come into the classroom. Some suggestions may include asking storytellers or authors to share stories; persons from the city or community to discuss summer activities; a local news team or member to discuss news, production, and reporting; and local people to discuss student-selected topics of interest. Someone could come to speak about the available local volunteer opportunities. They might give your class or school some exciting press coverage. Some good end-of-the-year school news can only help.

Another suggestion may be to plan *sponge* (filler) activities that may help keep the students interested in subject area learning. Sponge activities can be found on the Internet at the following location:

Scholastic.com: **http://www.scholastic.com/teachers/article/classroom-activities-sponge-ideas-grades-k%C2%965**

You can borrow ideas from other teachers. Nelson and Bailey (2008, p. 33) share some sponge ideas:

- Write the names of the states in alphabetical order.
- List all of the countries you can remember.
- Calculate the number of fingers and toes in our class.
- List all the ways we use math in our lives.
- Write as many words as you can think of that are derived from the root word life.
- List pairs of rhyming words.

In addition to thinking about how to keep instruction up and running at the end of the year, teachers must think about the management that must continue to the last day of school. Rewards, recognitions, and catch-them-being-good strategies must still be an active part of your classroom management. Individual and group goals and rewards are necessary to keep the students actively engaged in the learning process to the very end.

It seems the last days are even more hectic when the schedule changes. Often books have been collected and the students are without textbooks for these last days. Sometimes special classes such as music, art, and physical education are stopped one to two weeks before school ends. This means the students are with you more of the time. It is important to continue to enforce the same management plan that you started with the first of the year. You may want to use student input to direct the selection of the final two-week plan of study. One first-year teacher remarked about year-end planning, "I didn't want the day or the bell to end my first year; I wanted to end it my way." Yes, you have the challenge of composing the ending of your first-year experience.

Plan Projects

Several veteran classroom teachers suggest the following ideas to sustain students' interest and enthusiasm in school and in your classroom during the final days.

In preparing these end-of-the-year projects, start your planning about three to four weeks prior to the end of school. Use the same lesson plan outline form (see Figure 5.1) and the same management plan format described in Chapter 5.

Individual Work Projects

Assign individual work projects to students to complete on their own. Two projects are suggested below:

1. **Independent review packets.** Students complete review sheets for one or more subjects.

2. **Independent Learning Unit** (ILU). (See the following example.)

Topic: Seven US Regions

Each student receives a file folder with a blank US map stapled to the inside. The student decorates the folder cover to depict the contents of the folder.

Each folder contains a cover sheet with a list of activities to be completed in a week. Introduce the unit on Monday; Tuesday and Wednesday, students work independently; on Thursday check the folder; and give a quiz on Friday. Students can work on units any time, such as before and after assemblies or when the teacher needs to work on end-of-year checklist procedures.

The following activities might be included in the file folders:

a. Locate and label states and their capitals on your US map.

b. Describe each region.

c. Locate rivers and mountain ranges.

d. Choose a state, cite interesting facts, and describe its importance.

e. Draw a poster advertising a state or region.

f. Complete chapter questions or worksheets.

g. Categorize items about the region.

h. Make graphs of the state, regional, or national statistics.

i. Prepare oral presentations.

Group Work Projects

Assign group work projects to groups of students to complete together. Four projects are described below:

1. **Create books for the class library** (writing, illustrating, and binding). The teacher will need to get parents and guardians to help and a librarian or resource teacher to demonstrate bookmaking. Guest speakers during the unit may be authors, illustrators, and publishers. Students can work in pairs or groups. Students can read their books to other classes.

2. **Design a study guide for new students.** This activity is a good review of the curriculum. Form cooperative learning groups and assign each group a subject area. Compile all the information into a grade-level study guide for new students. Students could also create a *Guidebook for New Students*, which may be very helpful if moving into a new school.

3. **Develop a booklet or pamphlet such as "Everything You Need to Know About Sixth Grade to Survive and Be Successful."** This can be developed for any grade level. Use cooperative learning groups to plan, develop, and write the booklet or pamphlet. Assign tasks within the group; compile essential information; and design, illustrate, and bind the booklet. Students can share booklets or pamphlets with each other or other classes.

4. **Write an end-of-the-year newsletter.** The newsletter idea was developed initially in the 30-day management plan (see Chapter 5). This particular end-of-the-year edition could include subject reviews; class overviews; changes for next year; awards, assemblies, and recognition information; interviews with first-year teachers; advice for next year; and student plans for the summer.

Related Projects

Related projects can be from an interest area, a subject area, or may include two or more subject areas. The projects are usually integrated under a theme and can be completed independently or in groups. Three projects are presented below:

1. **Create time capsules.** Time capsules are designed by each student to contain memorabilia of the school year, such as headlines depicting interesting, noteworthy events; items of interest; review sheets of the curriculum; and advice or success stories. The container itself must be designed by the student. When the time capsule is completed, the student can bury or hide it. The student then draws a map leading to the capsule and gives it to the teacher.

2. **Teach a lesson.** Students choose their favorite subject and plan and teach a lesson to the class. This will give them an opportunity to be creative and innovative and will keep students engaged in learning activities even at the end of the year.

3. **Create a yearbook.** In her book **The Teacher's Guide to Success**, Kronowitz (2012, pp. 468–469), mentions that the end of the year is a time to create memories. She suggests the class create a PowerPoint presentation with an autobiographical slide for each student to make a miniyearbook.

Other project ideas are as follows:

- Have your students read stories to kindergartners or first-graders.
- Plan cross-age tutor-partner time.

- Have students pick a topic or hobby and share it with the class in a creative way.

- Have students report on their favorite book and compile a class list titled "Most Wanted Books." Include a summary and a line or two for rating each book.

- Have your current students write letters to the next group of students. The letters are a great way to begin your next school year.

- Have students use technology to provide a survival guide for next year's students.

II. End-of-the-Year Management Plan

The Last Three Weeks

Goal: End the Year With Confidence

Key Teaching Areas

- ❏ Continue to teach management plan.

- ❏ Maintain routines, cues, and procedures.

- ❏ Introduce projects.

- ❏ Discuss expectations.

Strategies for Success

- ❏ Prepare students for learning units.

- ❏ Intersperse introduction of learning units within daily schedule.

- ❏ Present resource material or people.

With three weeks of school remaining, use week 1 to prepare students for selecting learning units for the end-of-year activities. Use weeks 2 and 3 to teach the selected units. The following is a plan for the five days of week 1.

Day 1—Plan for Success

BEGIN THE DAY: Teacher and student greeter meet the students in the morning.

ROUTINE PROCEDURE: The routine procedure every morning is for the students to first get prepared for class upon entering the room and then to write in their journals for ten minutes.

OPENING ACTIVITY: Ask students to word web what they would like to learn in the remaining weeks of school. Explain that suggestions must be realistic but creative, different, and fun. List the suggestions on the board under the heading, "Ideas for Learning." The teacher can add a few to the list. Discuss the ideas and learning opportunities. Students can then reduce the list and select several ideas. Place students into Think-Pair-Share teams or groups to begin developing ideas. After sharing, collect their ideas.

USE CUE: Raise your hand and move to the front of the room to get the students' attention. You may need, once again, to monitor the amount of time it takes to get everyone's attention. If students take too much time, take time from them to reinforce this procedure.

ACTIVITY: Continue with scheduled curriculum lesson plans.

AFTER-LUNCH ROUTINE: Specialized time for preparing the students for the end-of-the-year projects. This may be scheduled time for additional preparation or planning of the projects.

ACTIVITY: Continue with lesson plans.

END-OF-THE-DAY ROUTINE: Closure–read the selected Ideas for Learning. Suggest that students bring in more ideas for the projects.

REMINDERS:

   ✓ Remember marble jar for group rewards.

Day 2—Teach That "Effort Equals Outcome"

BEGIN THE DAY: Teacher and student greeter meet the students in the morning.

ROUTINE PROCEDURE: The morning routine procedure is for students to get ready for class upon entering the room and then to write in their journals for ten minutes.

OPENING ACTIVITY: Ask students for additional suggestions and ideas they've thought about for the projects. Record them on a list that you are keeping to plan the learning units.

USE CUE: Raise your hand and move to the front of the room to get the students' attention.

ACTIVITY: Continue with scheduled curriculum lesson plans.

AFTER-LUNCH ROUTINE: Specialized time for preparing the students for the end of the year projects. Provide specific information or materials.

ACTIVITY: Continue with curriculum lesson plans.

END-OF-THE-DAY ROUTINE: Ask the students to tell you one thing they learned today, one thing they relearned today, or one thing they will enjoy about the projects.

REMINDERS:

> ✓ Plan and prepare projects.
>
> ✓ Get file folders.

Day 3—Learning Can Be Fun

BEGIN THE DAY: Teacher and student greeter meet the students in the morning.

ROUTINE PROCEDURE: The morning routine procedure is for students to first get ready for class upon entering the room and then to write in their journals for ten minutes about the projects.

OPENING ACTIVITY: Students share more ideas about possible projects. List the ideas on the board. The students vote on the projects they would like for the remaining two weeks of class. Discuss whether this is a realistic number of projects. Have they selected too many? Review selections and vote again. Majority rules and the projects have been selected. List the winners on the front board.

USE CUE: Raise your hand and move to the front of the room to get the students' attention. You may need, once again, to monitor the amount of time it takes to get everyone's attention. If students take too much time, take time from students to reinforce this procedure.

GUIDELINES: Review the Guidelines for Giving Directions (see Chapter 5, page 106). The students may be working independently on some projects and in groups on other selected project ideas. Set up two scenarios of this procedure and ask students what step is missing. Ask why procedures are important to the success of the projects.

ACTIVITY: Continue with scheduled lesson plans.

AFTER-LUNCH ROUTINE: Specialized time for preparing the students for the end of the year and the projects. This may be scheduled time for additional preparation or planning of the projects. Resource speakers may also be planned. You can collect support information to share at this time or students may begin to read books pertaining to the project topics.

ACTIVITY: Continue with curriculum lesson plans.

END-OF-THE-DAY ROUTINE: Closure–How can you contribute to the success of the projects? What are some ideas that may be helpful when working together?

REMINDERS:

> ✓ Catch them being good!
>
> ✓ Pass out candy treats.

Day 4—Plan for the End of the Year as if It Were the Beginning

BEGIN THE DAY: Teacher and student greeter meet the students in the morning.

ROUTINE PROCEDURE: The morning routine procedure is for students to get ready for class upon entering the room and to write in their journals for ten minutes. Choose a topic related to the selected projects.

OPENING ACTIVITY: Students brainstorm ideas regarding the selected projects. Take each project and do a word web of ideas. Have students copy the webs to refer to later. The students may need to be assigned to cooperative learning groups for specific work assignments.

USE CUE: Raise your hand and move to the front of the room to get the students' attention.

GUIDELINES: The teacher reviews LEAP into Learning Together rules (see Chapter 5, page 116). The students will work and learn together during some of the selected projects, and these rules (expectations) for group interaction need to be discussed, modeled, and reinforced.

ACTIVITY: Continue with scheduled curriculum lesson plans.

AFTER-LUNCH ROUTINE: This may be scheduled time for students to plan the projects.

ACTIVITY: Continue with curriculum lesson plans.

END-OF-THE-DAY ROUTINE: Ask students, "Why are we practicing LEAP into Learning Together?"

REMINDERS:

- ✓ Set up a calendar or schedule to organize the selected projects.
- ✓ Make copies of Guidelines for Giving Directions and LEAP into Learning Together rules for groups to place in the file folders.
- ✓ Prepare an agenda sheet. See day 5 under OPENING ACTIVITY.

Day 5—End With Dignity

On the Friday before the week the projects begin, prepare students to get involved with the first selected project.

BEGIN THE DAY: Teacher and student greeter meet the students in the morning.

ROUTINE PROCEDURE: The morning routine procedure is for students to get ready for class upon entering the room and to write for ten minutes in their journals.

OPENING ACTIVITY: Pass out the file folder to plan the project. Distribute and discuss the calendar or schedule for students to record working time for the project. Develop time lines for the assignments and activities. Place the calendar or schedule in each project file folder and collect. Put the folder where students can access it and return it to the same location each day. Design an agenda sheet for the students to complete each day to note progress, note where they left off, and establish plans for the next day. All materials stay in the folder. Students may need to bring in a box to keep information, supplies, and materials.

USE CUE: Raise your hand and move to the front of the room to get the students' attention.

ACTIVITY: Continue with scheduled curriculum lesson plans.

AFTER-LUNCH ROUTINE: Read aloud to students or provide time for sustained silent reading (SSR).

ACTIVITY: Continue with curriculum lesson plans.

END-OF-THE-DAY ROUTINE: Ask students, "What can we learn from our projects? Why is this learning important?"

REMINDERS:

✓ Make a progress sheet to staple inside the cover of file folder.

For the next two weeks, continue with your lesson plans and facilitate the student projects. In week 3, or the last week of school, have students present their projects to class. Invite parents and guardians to attend the presentations. Create special certificates for each student. You can use online certificate generators (**www.aspen treemedia.com**) or you can create your own with Word or Publisher.

Planning for the end of the school year can reduce the deterioration of academic performance and bring a strong sense of closure to the first year of teaching (Merrill, 1991).

III. Reflecting on the First Year

When it comes to teaching, we often hear the overused adage, "Experience is the best teacher." Reflection augments your teaching experience and helps you become the best teacher. All first-year teachers need to reflect on their rookie year to prepare for the next year. Reflection is part of the practice of teaching. Reflecting on one's teaching provides an opportunity to evaluate, rethink, and chart a new course of action in achieving goals. Reflection is purposeful and can be considered a problem-solving approach to evaluating one's teaching and making improvements. Further, reflection can help teachers "have control over the content and processes of their own work" (Zeichner & Liston, 1996, p. 26).

First-year teaching experiences are powerful and influence the teacher's practice and attitude throughout their teaching careers (Kuzmic, 1994). In the book **Teaching in the Real World** by Zukergood and Bettencourt (2009, p. 225), Bettencourt, a first-year teacher, writes to her college professor in her journal about the need to cultivate self-reflection by saying "it is a technique you will use the rest of your teaching life." In her last journal entry she writes, "I guess if learning is a lifelong process, so is learning to teach." As shown here, journal writing can prepare teachers to practice self-examination and can even lead one to become philosophical about the practice of teaching.

Zeichner and Liston (1996, p. 6) discuss the five key features of a reflective teacher.

A reflective teacher

- examines, frames, and attempts to solve the dilemmas of classroom practice;

- is aware of and questions the assumptions and values he or she brings to teaching;

- is attentive to the institutional and cultural contexts in which he or she teaches;

- takes part in curriculum development and is involved in school change efforts; and

- takes responsibility for his or her own professional development.

Reflection allows the first-year teacher to enter, explore, and examine the world of professional growth and development. The majority of beginning teachers surveyed were unable to find enough time for reflection during their first year. It is important to make a commitment to becoming more of a reflective teacher in your second year of teaching. One first-year teacher commented that "reflecting is critical to our profession, and I really enjoyed that last day of the school year without students to reflect on the whole year." An experienced teacher was asked to comment on that statement and said, "I think reflection is wise and being wise is learning from our experiences." Teachers need to reflect on their teaching before, during, and after each year. Many teachers agree that through continued reflection, teaching skills grow and new skills develop that improve the practice of teaching (Stanulis, 1994).

Reflection is also an important part of the classroom management plan during your first year. Many teachers ask, "How do I find the time to reflect?" To find the time for reflection, it must be a top priority. Call it *My Time*. Mark a place for it in the plan book and condition yourself to routinely use this time for yourself. You will find that by establishing this habit and sticking to it, you will begin to feel its importance in helping you to feel on top of your teaching situation (instead of living with the fear it is on top of you).

Some teachers suggest that besides carving time out of a day or week to reflect, a teacher may want keep a teaching log or journal. The teacher can set aside as much as ten minutes of journal time each day as the children write in their journals. The format of a daily teaching log or journal might be as follows: (1) write a positive observation, (2) report an area of need, (3) develop two strategies that meet that need, and (4) identify a key word for the next day. In their book **Research in the Classroom**, Donoahue, Van Tassell, and Patterson (1996, pp. 11–13) describe a teacher who starts to keep a journal. She starts by writing the date and what she sees happening. Soon, she added a reflective statement or two on the significance of the occurrences. As she continued with the journal writing, she added a seating chart with large boxes for comments about individual students. Donoahue et al. discuss the five ways journal writing can facilitate reflective teaching. The authors feel journal writing can help a teacher be a bookkeeper, a detective, cheerleader, mentor or friend, and peer learner (pp. 16–29). Another format for a weekly journal or teaching log might be as follows: (1) write one thing you liked about the week, (2) identify one area that needs improvement, and (3) develop two strategies you plan to implement on Monday.

If writing in the teaching log or journal every day feels like an impossible task, you may have to be disciplined and establish one day a week to devote to this practice. For instance, you could designate Thursdays immediately after school for fifteen minutes as your uninterrupted journal time.

IV. How Do I Prepare for My Second Year?

Learning about one's teaching starts in the first year. The more you know about your *teaching self*, the more effective you are in the classroom (Bosch, 2006, p. 15). The practice of teaching is an on-going, lifelong learning adventure. The learning from the first year helps teachers prepare and be ready for the second year and the years to follow. Reflecting on the final days of your first-year experience, in particular, is important as it prepares and energizes you for the second year. Take the End-of-the-Year Reflection survey (see Figure 7.1) to help you think about your first year of teaching from the beginning to the end.

Let's take a look at a familiar last day scene:

> The last day of school has arrived. Both you and your students say your good-byes as their smiling faces race out the door. The classroom door closes and the

FIGURE 7.1   *Quick End-of-the-Year Reflection Survey*

1. How do I rate my first year?

    _____ Poor _____ Fair _____ Good _____ Great

2. What was my favorite subject to teach?

    _____ Math _____ English _____ Reading _____ Social Studies _____ Science

3. What was my least favorite subject to teach?

    _____ Math _____ English _____ Reading _____ Social Studies _____ Science

    Why?_____

4. List four activities that the students really enjoyed.

5. How did the kids like to work? _____ Independently _____ Pairs _____ Groups

6. Where do I need more management skills?

    _____ Behavioral problems   _____ Time on task

    _____ Classroom organization   _____ Grouping/cooperative learning

    _____ Differentiation   _____ Other (please specify)

7. How do I rate my teaching? _____ Poor _____ Fair _____ Good _____ Great

8. How do I rate my reflection? _____ Poor _____ Fair _____ Good _____ Great

9. List three management situations that I know I will handle differently next year.

10. List three new strategies that I want to use next year.

classroom is empty. The room is bare. There isn't even any noise. You look around and realize that you have completed your first year of teaching.

Reflection is a process that can empower and prepare you for the next time the classroom door opens and the students are back in their seats.

In preparation for your second year, show your growth by updating your portfolio and begin enriching the pages of your teaching life. It becomes, after the first year, a showcase of growth (Horton, 2004). Barrett (2000, p. 223) views the portfolio "as a tool for demonstrating teacher growth over time."

Zubizarreta (1994), focusing on the teaching portfolio as an evidence-based document, states "teaching portfolios are becoming perhaps the most effective tool in improving instruction of both new and seasoned teachers and in providing a supportive, convincing method of evaluation" (p. 323).

The first year is a year that will remain in your memory forever; however, the second year is a new year. Some veteran teachers provided advice for your second-year experience, and they still report the need to find support and network with others. They suggest you find, form, and join a support group. Some teachers mentioned forming a group that meets on a regular basis, such as one afternoon or evening each week. A few teachers commented that they set up a computer network with four or five teachers with whom they communicated each week at a designated time. This support becomes even more important in the second year of teaching, as it provides a way to get feedback and suggestions, as well as an opportunity to share successes and express frustrations.

The surveyed experienced teachers offered the following advice for your second year of teaching:

- Keep in touch with friends, colleagues, and university professors.

- Continue to keep a journal.

- Renew personal and professional goals.

- Practice OHIO–Only Handle It (Paper) Once. Do it now and get it done is your personal second-year motto.

- Join a health spa or develop an exercise program. Never sacrifice this time, for it is necessary to replenish an exhausted body and mind.

- Eat healthy foods and get plenty of sleep.

- Download several songs that you enjoy hearing or singing. Listen to them in the car on the way to work.

- Smile, stay positive and idealistic, and continue to believe in yourself. You must become your own advocate.

- Subscribe to professional journals and attend professional conferences. Join professional organizations.

- Read books for pleasure as well as professional books.

- Remember even veteran teachers are anxious about the beginning and the ending of each school year.

- Relax, you have done this (once) before.

As you prepare for your second year of teaching, we hope you will begin to feel the excitement of challenging young minds and seeing children delight in their ability to learn and master, seek and find, and try and succeed. Our goal in writing this book was to prepare you for your *first* year of teaching and your *first* classroom of students. This book will continue to prepare you for all of your teaching years. We hope that with your first year behind you, you will be looking forward to embarking on another adventure—your **second year** of teaching. Students are our future, but then again, so are our teachers. The book began with asking "Where do I start," and now, you can say, "I am on my way"—herein tells the story of a teacher who moves from campus to classroom, and from being a beginner to a veteran.

REFERENCES

American Association for Employment in Education. (1997). *AAEE Job Search Handbook for Educators*. Columbus, OH: Author.

American Association for Employment in Education. (2015). *AAEE Job Search Handbook for Educators*. Columbus, OH: Author.

Anderson, L. W. (2004). *Increasing teacher effectiveness* (2nd ed.). Paris, France: UNESCO, International Institute for Educational Planning.

Anderson, L. W., & Krathwohl, D. (Eds.). (2001). A taxonomy for learning, teaching, and assessing: A revision of Bloom's taxonomy of educational objectives. Boston, MA: Allyn & Bacon.

Anthony, R., & Roe, G. (2003). *101 grade A résumés for teachers* (3rd ed.). Hauppauge, NY: Barron's Educational.

Barrett, H. (2000). *Electronic teaching portfolios: Multimedia skills + portfolio development = powerful professional development*. Retrieved from http://electronicportfolios.org/portfolios/site2000.html

Berla, N. (1992). Getting middle school parents involved. *Education Digest, 58*(2), 18–19.

Bloom, B. S. (1956). *Taxonomy of educational objectives: The classification of educational goals: Handbook I: Cognitive domain*. New York, NY: David McKay.

Bosch, K. A. (1991). Cooperative learning: Instruction and procedures to assist middle school teachers. *Middle School Journal, 22*(3), 34–35.

Bosch, K. A. (2006). *Planning classroom management* (2nd ed.). Thousand Oaks, CA: Corwin.

Bosch, K. A., & Kersey, K. C. (1993). Just be quiet and learn. *Clearing House, 66*(4), 229.

Bullough, R. V. (1989). *First-year teacher: A case study*. New York, NY: Teachers College Press.

Bullough, R. V., & Baughman, K. (1997). *First-year teacher eight years later: An inquiry into teacher development*. New York, NY: Teachers College Press.

Burrall, B. (2006, June). Time Savers. *Technology & Learning, 26*(8), 11.

Campbell, D. M., Melenyzer, B. J., Nettles, D. H., & Wyman, R. M., Jr. (2013). *How to develop a professional portfolio: A manual for teachers* (6th ed.). Boston, MA: Allyn & Bacon.

Compton-Lilly, C. (1999). Teacher researcher perspectives on parent involvement. *Journal for Teacher Research, 202*(2), 4–8.

Covey, S. R. (2004). *The 7 habits of highly effective people.* New York, NY: Simon & Schuster.

Cushman, S. (2004). What is co-teaching? In R. A. Villa, *A guide to co-teaching* (pp. 1–9). Thousand Oaks, CA: Corwin.

Davis, B. H., Resta, V., Knox, A., & Anderson, M. A. (1998). Voices from the classroom: Collaborative action research. *Proceedings of Partnership Conference.* Flagstaff: Northern Arizona University: Partnerships in Education.

Davis, B. H., Resta, V., Miller, K., & Fortman, K. (1999). Beginning teachers improve classroom practice through collaborative inquiry. *Journal for Teacher Research, 202*(2), 1–12.

Donoahue, Z., Van Tassell, M. A., & Patterson, L. (Eds.). (1996). *Research in the classroom: Talk, texts, and inquiry.* Newark, DE: International Reading Association.

Drayer, A. (1979). *Problems in middle and high school teaching.* Boston, MA: Allyn & Bacon.

Emmer, E. T., & Evertson, C. M. (2012). *Classroom management for middle and high school teachers* (9th ed.). Upper Saddle River, NJ: Pearson.

Epstein, J. L. (1994). Theory to practice: Schools and family partnerships lead to school improvement and student success. In C. L. Fagnano & B. Z. Werber (Eds.), *School, family, and community interaction: A view from the firing lines* (pp. 39–52). Boulder, CO: Westview.

Evertson, C. M., & Anderson, L. M. (1979). Beginning school. *Educational Horizons, 57,* 164–168.

Evertson, C. M., & Emmer, E. T. (2012). *Classroom management for elementary teachers* (9th ed.). Upper Saddle River, NJ: Pearson.

Good, T. L., & Brophy, J. (2007). *Looking in classrooms* (10th ed.). Boston, MA: Allyn & Bacon.

Gould, P. (1999). Parents are stepping out of their passive roles. *San Diego Business Journal, 20*(18), 2–6.

Grady, M. P. (1998). *Qualitative and action research: A practitioner handbook.* Bloomington, IN: Phi Delta Kappa.

Gruber, B., & Gruber, S. (2002, August/September). 6 quick tips for success. *Teaching K–8,* 80–81.

Halvorsen, A. T., & Neary, T. (2001). *Building inclusive schools: Tools and strategies for success.* Needham Heights, MA: Allyn & Bacon.

Henderson, A. T. (Ed.). (1987). *The evidence continues to grow: Parent involvement improves student achievement.* Columbia, MD: National Committee for Citizens in Education.

Henderson, A. T., Mapp, K. L., Johnson, V. R., & Davies, D. (2007). *Beyond the bake sale: The essential guide to family/school partnerships.* New York, NY: The New Press.

Hennick, C. (1999, August). 11 "magic" tricks for new teachers. *Instructor, 117*(1), 36–40.

Hiatt-Michael, D. B. (2001). Schools as learning communities: A vision for organic school reform. *School Community Journal, 11,* 93–112

Hoak, H. (1999). Reflections of a first-year teacher. *Reading Today, 17*(1), 18.

Horton, M. (2004, November/December). Digital portfolios in physical education teacher preparation. *Journal of Physical Education, Recreation and Dance, 75*(9), 35.

Hubbard, R. S., & Power, B. M. (1998). *Teacher research: The journal of classroom inquiry.* Albany, NY: Johnson Press.

Hunter, M. (1989). Join the "par-aide" in education. *Educational Leadership, 47*(2), 36–39.

Jennings, W. (1989). How to organize successful parent advisory committees. *Educational Leadership, 47*(2), 42–45.

Johns, K. M., & Espinoza, C. (1996). *Management strategies for culturally diverse classrooms.* Bloomington, IN: Phi Delta Kappa.

Keller, B. (2008). Schools seek to channel parent involvement. *Education Week, 27*(31), 1–17.

Kersey, K. C. (1990/1994). *Don't take it out on your kids.* Washington, DC: Acropolis Books.

Knowles, J. (1990). Understanding teaching perspectives. *Journal of Teacher Education, 41*(1), 28–38.

Kottler, E., Kottler, J. A., & Kottler, C. J. (2004). *Secrets for secondary school teachers: How to succeed in your first year* (2nd ed.). Thousand Oaks, CA: Corwin.

Kronowitz, E. L. (2012). *The teacher's guide to success* (2nd ed.). Boston, MA: Pearson.

Kuzmic, J. (1994). A beginning teacher's search for meaning: Teacher socialization, organizational literacy, and empowerment. *Teaching and Teacher Education, 10*(1), 15–27.

Lovette, O. K. (1996). From the trenches: First year teacher comments and perspectives. *College Student Journal, 30*(3), 302–306.

McDaniel, T. R. (1986). A primer on classroom discipline: Principles old and new. *Phi Delta Kappan, 68*, 63–68.

Merrill, A. (1991). Planning for the end of the year at a middle school. *Middle School Journal, 22*(5), 5–9.

Murawski, W. W., & Dieker, L. A. (2008). 50 ways to keep your co-teacher. *Teaching Exceptional Children, 40*(4), 40–48.

Nelson, K. J., & Bailey, K. (2008). *Starting strong: Surviving and thriving as a new teacher.* Thousand Oaks, CA: Corwin.

Parks, B. (1998, January/February). 7 Time-management sanity savers. *Instructor-Intermediate, 107*(5), 46.

Patterson, L., Baldwin, S., Gonzales, R., Guadarrams, I., & Keith, L. (1999). Claiming our ignorance, and making new friends: A different approach to family involvement. *Journal for Teacher Research, 202*(2), 1–10.

Pauly, E. (2002, December/January). No one told me about May. *Journal of Adolescent and Adult Literacy, 46*(4), 284.

Pedota, P. (2007, March/April). Strategies for effective classroom management in the secondary setting. *The Clearing House, 80*(4), 165.

Ribas, W. B. (1992). Helping teachers communicate with parents. *The Principal, 72*(2), 19–20.

Ribas, W. B. (1998). Tips for reaching parents. *Educational Leadership, 56*(1), 83–85.

Rooney, J. (2004). The first day of school. *Educational Leadership, 62*(1), 86–87.

Ryan, K. (Ed.). (1970). *Don't smile until Christmas.* Chicago, IL: University of Chicago Press.

Ryan, K. (Ed.). (1986). *The induction of new teachers.* Bloomington, IN: Phi Delta Kappa.

Salend, S. J. (2010). *Creating inclusive classrooms: Effective and reflective practices* (7th ed.). Upper Saddle River, NJ: Prentice Hall.

Sapon-Shevin, M. (1995). Building a safe community for learning. In W. Ayers, *To become a teacher: Making a difference in children's lives* (pp. 99–112). New York, NY: Teachers College Press.

Sapon-Shevin, M. (1999). *Because we can change the world: A practical guide to building cooperative, inclusive classroom communities.* Thousand Oaks, CA: Corwin.

Schell, L. M., & Burden, P. R. (2000). *Countdown to the first day of school: A K–12 get ready checklist for beginning teachers.* Washington, DC: National Education Association.

Shockley, B., Michalove, B., & Allen, J. (1995). *Engaging families: Connecting home and school literacy communities.* Portsmouth, NH: Heinemann.

Shumway, L. K., Gallo, G., Dickson, S., & Gibbs, J. (2011). *Co-teaching handbook: Utah guidelines.* Salt Lake City: Utah State Office of Education.

Sileo, J. M. (2005, August 2). *Co-teaching: Best practices for education.* Paper presented at Inclusive and Supportive Education Congress, International Special Education Conference, Inclusion: Celebrating Diversity. Glasgow, Scotland.

Sleeter, C. E., & Grant, C. A. (2008). *Making choices for multicultural education: Five approaches to race, class, and gender* (6th ed.). Hoboken, NJ: Wiley.

Smith, M. M. (1993). The beginning teacher's first month. *Kappa Delta Pi Record, 29*(4), 120–125.

Smith, T. E., Polloway, E., Patton, R., & Dowdy, C. A. (2007). *Teaching students with special needs in inclusive settings* (5th ed.). Boston, MA: Allyn & Bacon.

Stanulis, R. N. (1994, January). Fading to a whisper: One mentor's story of sharing her wisdom without telling answers. *Journal of Teacher Education, 45,* 31–38.

Stevens, B. A., & Tollafield, A. (2003). Creating comfortable and productive parent/teacher conferences. *Phi Delta Kappan, 84*(7), 523–524.

Strother, D. B. (1985). Practical applications of research: Classroom management. *Phi Delta Kappan, 66*(10), 723–728.

Thompson, B. (2008). Characteristics of parent-teacher e-mail communication. *Communication Education, 57*(2), 201–223.

Time savers for and from educators. (1995). *Education Digest, 61*(1), 31.

Tonnsen, S., & Patterson, S. (1992). Fighting first-year jitters. *The Executive Educator, 14*(1), 29–30.

Tucker, P. D., Stronge, J. H., & Gareis, C. R. (2002). *Handbook on teacher portfolios.* Larchmont, NY: Eye on Education.

Veenman, S. (1984, Summer). Perceived problems of beginning teachers. *Review of Educational Research, 54*(2), 155–174.

VGM Career Horizons. (2004). *Resumes for education careers.* Lincolnwood, IL: Author.

Weinstein, C., Curran, M., & Tomlinson-Clark, S. (2003, Autumn). Culturally responsive classroom management: Awareness into action. *Theory into Practice, 42*(4), 271.

Worthy, J. (2005, May/June). It didn't have to be so hard: The first years of teaching in an urban school. *International Journal of Qualitative Studies in Education, 18*(3), 379–398.

Zeichner, K. M., & Liston, D. P. (1996). *Reflective teaching: An introduction.* Mahwah, NJ: Lawrence Erlbaum.

Zeichner, K. M., & Wray, S. (2001). The teaching portfolio in US teacher education programs: What we know and what we need to know. *Teaching and Teacher Education, 17*(5), 614.

Zubizarreta, J. (1994). Teaching portfolios and the beginning teacher. *Phi Delta Kappan, 76*(4), 327.

Zukergood, D., & Bettencourt, A. (2009). *Teaching in the real world.* Upper Saddle River, NJ: Pearson.

Zuckerman, J. (2007, Spring). Classroom management in secondary schools: A study of student teachers' successful strategies. *American Secondary Education, 35*(2), 4–16.

INDEX

A SAGE Company

Corwin is committed to improving education for all learners by publishing books and other professional development resources for those serving the field of PreK–12 education. By providing practical, hands-on materials, Corwin continues to carry out the promise of its motto: **"Helping Educators Do Their Work Better."**

Made in the USA
San Bernardino, CA
19 January 2018